Shekinahglory Press

This book is a gift of love and light.
With Gratitude,

Shechinahglory Tucker

A Pure Heart with No Boundaries

A Journey of Healing, Dreams and Self-Compassion
By Shechinahglory E. Tucker
Shekinahglory Press

Narrative Disclaimer: This book is a personal memoir based on the author's dreams, life experiences, and spiritual reflections. While the events, interpretations, and emotions described are true to the author's perspective, some names, details, and sequences have been altered or combined for narrative clarity and creative expression. Any resemblance to actual people, living or dead, events, or locales outside the author's direct experience is purely coincidental.

Content Disclaimer: This book is intended for inspiration, reflection, and personal growth. It is not a substitute for professional mental health, medical, or legal advice. Any interpretations of dreams, symbols, or spiritual concepts are based on my personal beliefs and experiences. Readers are encouraged to seek professional guidance where appropriate and to interpret the content in a way that aligns with their own faith and discernment.

Published by Shekinahglory Press
Ridgeland, SC
www.shekinahglorypress.com

ISBN (Paperback): [979-8-9933616-0-4]

First Edition – 2025
Printed in the United States of America

Disclaimer: This book contains limited artistic depictions of nudity, presented only in a non-erotic, symbolic, and spiritual context.

Content Advisory

This book contains occasional artistic depictions of nudity. These images are presented in a non-erotic, non-pornographic context, intended solely for artistic, spiritual, and healing purposes.

The illustrations and descriptions are meant to reflect themes of vulnerability, identity, and wholeness. They are not included for sexual stimulation or explicit content, but rather as symbols of truth, healing, and self-expression.

Readers are encouraged to approach these images with an open heart, understanding that they are part of the author's journey of faith, growth, and transformation.

Dedication

For every soul walking between paradise and fire — may this work remind you that love never fails.
(Original art

Author's Note

This book is a personal work drawn from my own dreams, memories, and spiritual reflections.

Each chapter represents an authentic record of my experiences, as I remember and interpret them, paired with my thoughts, symbolic insights, and spiritual guidance.

While I have received creative and structural assistance in shaping these pages, the words, stories, and meanings are entirely my own.

They come from my heart, my journey, and my unique encounters — both in the waking world and the dream world.

I share them here with the hope that others may find connection, comfort, and understanding through their own reflections.

— Shechinahglory E. Tucker

Table of Contents

Introduction

Before you open this book, I want you to pause and take in the cover. Every image, every symbol you see carries a piece of my story — a story that began long before I even realized I was on a spiritual journey.

I didn't step into inner child healing, shadow work, or dream work by accident.

I was led here — pulled here — by God Himself. This path was given to me as part of my divine mission on this earth. I now know that my purpose is bigger than me: to awaken to who God created me to be, to walk in His light, and to live out the mission He has placed on my heart. But the road here was paved with heartbreak, betrayal, and lessons I never saw coming.

I have always been a giver — an earth angel — someone who loves deeply and with pure intentions. And yet, time and again, I found myself surrounded by people who could not or would not return that same love. Family, friends, coworkers, romantic partners… it didn't matter. The pattern was the same: I would pour my heart into them, and they would take more than they ever gave back.

At first, I didn't understand. Why did God make me this way if all it brought me was pain? But over time, I realized that givers and takers are both placed on this earth to teach each other lessons. For me, the lesson was about boundaries. My heart is my greatest gift — but it is not meant to be handed out without wisdom.

The art on this cover was born years ago, before I could put these lessons into words. Back then, I didn't fully understand what I was feeling. I just drew it. Now, fifteen years later, after living through the storms that would shape me, I can see exactly what that artwork was trying to tell me.

At the top of the image, the word "PARADISE" rests above the cross and sunlight. This is God — the Divine Creator, the source of all light and love. Beneath it, a crown on a heart represents me: the earth angel, a divine being from God. The crown sits on the heart because no matter how many times my heart is pierced or broken, I still choose to wear it with honor and love others openly.

Inside that crown are the words "S.E.T 4 Life" — initials for my name, Shechinahglory Elisheba Tucker. As a child, I would write this everywhere without fully knowing why. Now I see it as a sign from God: a reminder that He is always with me, that I am blessed, and that I will always be provided for. Even the meaning of my name carries divine weight — Shechinahglory meaning "God's promise" and the divine feminine presence of God: mother, nurturer, protector, and compassionate one. Elisheba meaning "God is my oath" and "God is my abundance." God alone led my parents to give me these names, and through them He confirmed that I am held and guided by Him.

Then there's "LOVE" inside a heart pierced by an arrow. This is my reminder that I am human. My heart can break. I can be betrayed, stabbed in the back, and left bleeding. In the art, that blood transforms into water, pouring out to extinguish the "Hate on Flames" at the bottom. Even through hate, chaos, and cruelty, I still pour love into the world — even to those who have hurt me.

Surrounding the heart are other symbols:

Basketball and track — reminders of earthly joys, grounding me between heaven and hell. These sports were passions of mine, symbols of movement, discipline, and expression while living on earth.

The numbers 5 and 7 — when I drew this art at 15 years old, these numbers only reflected my favorite basketball players: Kevin Garnett (5) and Carmelo Anthony (7). Now, their meaning runs deeper. Spiritually, number 5 speaks to embracing spiritual growth, making positive changes, and stepping into freedom under divine guidance. The number 7 is heavenly — a symbol of perfection, eternal life, and the truth that the strongest spiritual growth often comes under pressure. Both remind me that God will never put me through anything I cannot bear.

But here's the truth I had to face: every time I gave away my divine energy to people who didn't value it, they would walk away healed, lighter, maybe even better than they were before meeting me — while I was left drained and in need of my own healing. It took years to understand that God wasn't punishing me. He was teaching me. Every heartbreak was a lesson in protecting my love, in giving with discernment, in placing sacred boundaries around the energy He gave me.

This book is about that journey — about the duality of life: Heaven and hell. Love and hate. Light and darkness.
It's about meeting your inner child, facing your shadow self, and stepping into the divine purpose God created for you.
So, as you read these pages, I invite you to see yourself in my story.
I invite you to heal.

And I invite you to walk into your own Paradise with your heart crowned, your spirit whole, and your boundaries strong.

Chapter 1 When God Speaks Through Heartbreak
Learning to Put Myself First Without Guilt

I didn't just wake up one day and decide to give more than I received — it was something planted in me long before I understood what it meant.

Growing up, I was surrounded by love. My mother and family loved me deeply, and from them I learned how to love without holding back. I was taught to be giving, caring, and attentive to others — to help when I could and to treat people the way I wanted to be treated.
Over time, I carried that same heart into my friendships, my jobs, and my romantic relationships. I believed that if I loved hard enough, if I gave without limits, people would value that love and cherish me in return. What I didn't realize then was that I was showing others I would always give, even if it cost me pieces of myself.
That's how I walked straight into one of the most painful chapters of my life.

I had been through storms before, but nothing like the hurricane I endured in those two years with my past lover — a karmic tie, a narcissist, wrapped in charm.
In the beginning, she was everything I thought I wanted. Sweet. Attentive. Kind. We could talk for hours until the sun came up. She seemed to know my thoughts before I spoke them, finishing my sentences like we shared the same soul. We spoiled each other with gifts. She told me she wanted everything I wanted — real estate, investing in cryptocurrency, stocks, bonds, buying a home, building a family. It sounded perfect.

But deep in my spirit, I felt something was off. God whispered to me in the quiet, but I ignored His voice. I followed my desire for the picture-perfect life we painted together. I clung to the dream instead of the truth.

As time passed, cracks began to show. The things we dreamed about weren't her dreams at all — they were lies. And as she revealed more pieces of her life, God revealed more truth to me. Still, I ignored Him. I didn't want to believe that the person I loved was not who she claimed to be.

The relationship became a slow bleed. Emotionally, spiritually, mentally, physically, financially — she drained me dry. No matter how much I gave, it was never enough. She was selfish, spiteful, manipulative, deceitful. And I... I was losing myself.

I threw myself into work just to escape the tension at home. I avoided her to avoid the arguments. I used to be joyful, lighthearted, and full of life — but this relationship dimmed my light until I was a shadow of myself. It felt like I was crawling through my days, dragging my soul behind me.

And I wasn't perfect either. The constant bickering pushed me out of character. I hate arguing, but she seemed to feed on it. I would walk away just to keep my peace, but she would chase after my anger. She wanted to see me break, and sometimes... I did.

My family and friends began asking me what was wrong. Even when I smiled, they could see it — the weight had settled into my face. I told them I was fine, but I wasn't. I was drowning, and I didn't even realize how deep I was under.

And yet, I stayed. Because deep down, I still loved her. I still looked forward to coming home to her after being on the road. Until one day... I came home to find her with someone else, already replacing me.

The rage that rose in me that day — I can't even describe it. I packed up and left, but my heart was shattered into pieces too small to gather.

In the weeks after, I questioned God over and over.

Why did you let me meet her? Why would you place someone in my life who would destroy so much of me? What was the point?

I didn't expect an answer to come from her lips. But one day, we crossed paths again. She looked me in the eyes and said, "You're a really good person... but you just need to learn to put yourself first."

At the time, her words felt like noise. I didn't want to hear anything from her, not after all the pain she caused. But later, I realized — that was my answer.

God had spoken through the very person who hurt me. My purpose in that relationship wasn't to save her or build a dream together. It was to learn the lesson I had ignored for years: Put yourself first.

God knows my heart. He knows my caretaker instinct. He knows how easily I put everyone else's needs ahead of my own peace. And in His infinite wisdom, He used my deepest heartbreak to teach me the truth I needed to carry into the rest of my life.

Reflection: God Speaks Even Through the Pain

Sometimes the most powerful messages from God don't come wrapped in beauty — they come from the very source of our hurt. It can feel unfair, even cruel, but when we quiet our hearts and listen, we realize He is answering the prayers we prayed in our deepest confusion.

The same person you thought broke you may be the one God used to break the cycle that was hurting you.

When God tells you to put yourself first, it's not selfishness — it's protection. It's the starting point for the life He has called you to live.

Your Turn to Reflect

Scriptures to Meditate On:
Proverbs 4:23 – Above all else, guard your heart, for everything you do flows from it.

Romans 8:28 – And we know that in all things God works for the good of those who love him, who have been called according to his purpose.

Isaiah 41:10 – So do not fear, for I am with you; do not be dismayed, for I am your God. I will strengthen you and help you; I will uphold you with my righteous right hand.

Reflection Questions:

Has God ever spoken to you through pain? Describe what happened and how it shaped you.

_____

_____

_____

_____

_____

Where have you ignored your intuition or God's voice in your life?

_____

_____

_____

_____

What would "putting yourself first" look like for you today — without guilt?

_____

_____

_____

_____

Closing Prayer:

Lord,

Thank You for loving me enough to protect me, even when I didn't understand it at the time. Teach me to guard my heart and to put myself first in a way that honors You. Help me hear Your voice above my fears and give me the strength to walk away from anything that steals my peace.

Amen.

CHAPTER ONE

Heart Check-In

Think about your last relationship or situation that broke your heart. On the left, write down what you poured into it. On the right, write down what you actually received back. Let this exercise show you the truth.

What I gave	What I received
Love I poured in	How they responded
Time I sacrificed	What I felt in return
Energy I used	What I lacked
Support I offered	What was taken from me

Lord, help me to see the truth in my patterns of love.

♥

God's Whisper vs. My Desire

Sometimes we choose desire over wisdom. Write down the whispers of God you felt but ignored, and then what you chased instead. This helps you see where you placed your hope versus where God was guiding you.

God's Whispers I Ignored

(e.g., "This doesn't feel right." "Pay attention to the red flags." "Be still.")

_____
_____
_____
_____
_____
_____

What I Chose Instead

(e.g., "Believed their promises." "Stayed because I was afraid to be alone." "Clung to the fantasy.")

_____
_____
_____
_____
_____
_____

 Listening to God is choosing protection, not punishment.

The Mirror Letter

Write a letter to yourself as if you were your own best friend.

Speak life into yourself the way you would encourage someone you love.

I admire you for...

_____

I forgive you for...

_____

You deserve love
that feels like...

_____

I promise to...

_____

I am my own safe place.

Release Ritual

Write down the name(s) of anyone who has hurt you and what you need to release. When you're done, pray over it, tear it out, or speak it out loud. This is your step toward freedom.

Write their name here

_____

What I need to release is...

_____

What I'm choosing to keep
(lessons, wisdom, strength)...

_____

_____

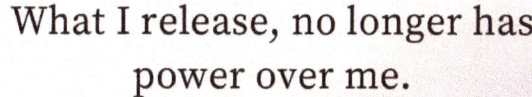

What I release, no longer has
power over me.

Self-Care Commitment Contract

This is your sacred contract between you and God to choose

yourself. Fill it in, sign it, and remember it every time you're
tempted to put others before your peace

I will guard my heart by...

_____

_____

I will listen to God's e by...

_____

_____

I will put myself first by...

_____

_____

♥ Signed with love, _____

I am worthy of the love I give so freely.

Boundary Building Map

Your peace is sacred. Protect it by setting boundaries in each

area of your life. Boundaries are not walls — they are doors
that teach others how to love you.

Time

e.g. I won't give
all my free time
away.

_____

My Peace

_____

Energy
e.g. I won't explain
myself over over.

Finances
e.g. I won't let
others drain me

financially.

_____

Body

e.g. I won'tallow
toxic intimacy.

_____

Spirit
e.g.I won't ignore
when God says
leave.

_____

_____

_____

_____

_____

Boundaries protect what God placed inside me.

Chapter 2: Truth Overcoming a Fantasy

The Beginning

I did not listen to the words of my karmic ex that God used to talk to me about myself and the lesson I was supposed to learn. Instead, I met someone new. She was a lovely, beautiful woman with a smile that could light up a room.

When she walked into my life, it was as if the room itself shifted. Her smile didn't just light up the space — it reached inside of me, pulling me out of the shadows I had been sitting in for far too long. There was something about her presence that felt familiar, like a memory I couldn't place but had been waiting for my whole life to remember.

I had been through heartbreak before, but with her, it felt different. Every laugh, every glance, every touch seemed to carry weight — as if the universe itself had conspired to place us in the same moment at the same time. I didn't just see her; I felt her in my spirit. From the start, there was no denying that something powerful was unfolding.

I gave to her freely, not because I had to, but because my heart couldn't resist. The way she carried her pain reminded me of my own, and I thought maybe, just maybe, I had found someone who truly understood the language of my soul. She wasn't just another chapter — she felt like the entire book I had been searching for.

The more time we spent together, the deeper that feeling grew. When I was with her, the world faded. The chaos of life, the heaviness of my past, the scars I carried — none of it mattered when she was near. She had a way of making everything feel lighter, brighter, almost magical.
I remember the way her laughter could soften even my hardest days. The way her eyes seemed to hold galaxies, pulling me into them like gravity. The simplest moments with her — riding in the car, sitting together in silence, sharing late-night conversations — felt like the most extraordinary gifts. She wasn't just a woman to me; she was warmth, safety, fire, and peace all at once.

At first, she seemed like a blessing. I saw her struggling, going through a hard part in her life — one I knew all too well because I had lived through the same kind of trauma. And being who I am, leading with my big heart, I stepped in. I gave without boundaries, the way I always had. I poured into her with the same love and energy I had given to past lovers and to so many people in my life.

I thought this time would be different.

The Bond

As time went on, we grew closer. We laughed, shared stories, and went on dates. Because of her situation, I carried the weight of providing — paying for everything, wanting to make things easier for her. And then, one day, she looked at me and said something that stopped me in my tracks: "You feel like my person."

Those words stunned me. Shocked me. Deep down, I felt the same way — but the scars from my past and the mixed signals she sent made me question if I could trust it.

Her words said one thing, but her actions said another leaving me confused and aching. One moment she was all over me, showering me with affection, and the next she was distant, cold, unreachable. Some days she answered my calls; other days she let them ring unanswered. She told me what she wanted to do for me, how she wanted to give back for all I had done during her rough patch — but those promises never came to life.

Still, I held on. Because in between the chaos, there were moments of closeness that felt real. We bonded over our pain, over the betrayals and heartbreaks of past lovers, over the patterns of narcissism we had both endured. It felt like she understood me in a way few people ever had.

And I thought maybe, just maybe, this was finally it.

Ghosting

Eventually, she told me she had to move away because she couldn't make things work where she was — at least, that's what she said. But then, she ghosted me. She stopped responding to my texts and calls when I checked on her. She blocked me from social media.

I can't explain the kind of pain that brings. To pour so much of yourself into someone, to carry their burdens, to give love without limits — only for them to vanish without warning, without explanation.

I replayed everything in my mind, searching for what I had done wrong. What had I missed? What had I done to deserve to be abandoned like that? I found myself chasing her, desperate for clarity, desperate for closure.

And when I finally had the chance to speak to her again, her words cut like a knife: "Leave me alone."

The sting of rejection was sharp, but the confusion hurt even more. How could someone who once called me "her person" now want nothing to do with me?

The Search for Answers

In my confusion and heartbreak, I found myself searching for answers wherever I could. I even reached out to psychics, clinging to anything that might explain the silence. They told me she would reach out again. That she would contact me. That she was my twin flame.

Over and over, those words gave me hope.

But reality? The last time we spoke, she told me she didn't want to be with me and that I should leave her alone.

That cut deep. And still, I held on to what others said instead of her own words. I wanted to believe the fantasy more than the truth.

But here's what I've learned — and what I want you to hear too: truth is the only thing that sets you free.

Lessons From Pain

Twin Flame vs. God's Plan

The idea of a twin flame can feel powerful and magnetic, but sometimes it keeps us trapped in something God never intended for us to hold on to. Even if you share something meaningful with someone, not every connection is meant to last forever.

Some people come into our lives to reveal what we still need to heal, to show us where we still lack boundaries, or to push us closer to God. That doesn't make the bond meaningless — it makes it purposeful.

God reminds us in Jeremiah 29:11 that He has "plans to prosper you and not to harm you, plans to give you hope and a future." If someone has chosen a different path, trust that God is not removing them to punish you, but to protect you and prepare you for what He truly has ahead.

Respecting Boundaries as God's Protection

When someone tells you to leave them alone, it may sting, but sometimes God uses their words to give you clarity. What feels like rejection is often divine redirection.

Respecting boundaries doesn't mean you weren't worthy — it means God is showing you that your worth is far too great to keep begging for love that isn't freely given. By honoring their "no," you are honoring God's "yes" to your healing.

Proverbs 4:23 says it clearly: "Above all else, guard your heart, for everything you do flows from it." Respecting boundaries is one of the ways you guard your heart and allow God to heal what others broke.

The Danger of False Hope vs. God's Truth

When you're hurting, it's easy to cling to any voice that promises comfort — whether from psychics, friends, or even your own thoughts. They may tell you, "They'll come back," but God is not the author of confusion.

False hope can chain you to a door that He has already closed. Real peace begins when you stop chasing their "maybe" and start trusting God's clear "no."

In Isaiah 41:10, God says: "Do not fear, for I am with you... I will strengthen you and help you; I will uphold you with my righteous right hand." The hope you need isn't in whether they return — it's in knowing God will never leave you nor forsake you.

Shifting Focus Back to God and Your Purpose

The most powerful shift after heartbreak is taking all the energy you once poured into another person and surrendering it back to God. He can redirect it into your healing, your calling, your dreams, your relationships, and your destiny.

Letting go doesn't mean you are lost. It means you are making space for the blessing God has prepared for you. In fact, sometimes He has to clear the space in your heart so the person aligned with His will for your life can finally step in.

Romans 8:28 reminds us: "And we know that in all things God works for the good of those who love him, who have been called according to his purpose." Even this heartbreak is working for your good.

Facing Reality

I want to be tender yet gentle with this truth.

When someone expresses that they don't want a relationship and asks for space, it can be one of the hardest things to accept. Your heart may resist, and others may encourage you to hold on, but their words and actions are often God's way of showing you what is real. It doesn't mean you weren't worthy of love — it simply means God is guiding you toward a truth that will free and protect your heart.

That truth broke me. I wrestled with it, questioning why God allowed me to feel so deeply for someone who would turn away. I held onto hope, imagining maybe things could turn around. I believed the fantasy instead of facing the reality God was already showing me.

But here's what I've learned — and what I want you to hear too: God's truth will always set you free. Jesus said in John 8:32: "Then you will know the truth, and the truth will set you free."

Moving Forward

This is a painful place to be in, I know. The ache of rejection is real. The silence of someone you cared for can echo louder than words. But God will not waste your pain.

Instead of waiting on someone who doesn't want to stay, you can choose to pour that same energy into your walk with God. Into becoming the person, He created you to be. Into relationships that reflect His love. Into your calling, your dreams, your projects. Into new connections that God sends into your life — people who won't run but will align with His purpose for you.

Sometimes, when you finally let go, you create the very space that allows God to bring in the one who is truly aligned with your heart and destiny.

Your Turn to Reflect

Scriptures to Meditate On
Jeremiah 29:11 – "For I know the plans I have for you," declares the Lord, "plans to prosper you and not to harm you, plans to give you hope and a future."

Proverbs 4:23 – "Above all else, guard your heart, for everything you do flows from it."
Isaiah 41:10 – "Do not fear, for I am with you; do not be dismayed, for I am your God. I will strengthen you and help you; I will uphold you with my righteous right hand."

Romans 8:28 – "And we know that in all things God works for the good of those who love him, who have been called according to his purpose."

John 8:32 – "Then you will know the truth, and the truth will set you free."

Reflection Questions

Looking back, were there times when God was showing you the truth, but you chose to believe the fantasy?

_____
_____
_____
_____
_____
_____

How can you begin to see rejection not as abandonment, but as God's redirection?

_____

_____

_____

_____

_____

In what ways can you honor your worth and guard your heart more intentionally?

_____

_____

_____

_____

_____

What promises of God can you cling to when the voices of false hope get louder than His truth?

_____

_____

_____

_____

_____

How can you redirect your energy back into your relationship with God, your healing, and your divine purpose?

_____

_____

_____

_____

_____

_____

_____

_____

_____

_____

Closing Prayer
Heavenly Father,

Thank You for being the God of truth, the God who never leaves nor forsakes me. Lord, I confess that I have often clung to fantasies, false hopes, and broken promises instead of standing on Your Word. Forgive me for placing my hope in people more than in You. Teach me to respect the boundaries You reveal, to release what You have not willed, and to trust that Your plan is always better than mine. Heal my heart where it has been broken, redirect my steps where they have strayed, and fill me with the peace that surpasses all understanding. Help me to walk in truth, to let go with grace, and to embrace the future You have already written for me.

In Jesus' name, Amen.

Red Flags Reality Check

In each color zone, list behaviors from past relationships.

Green = actions that showed love & respect. Yellow = moments that gave mixed signals. Red = actions that clearly hurt or disrespected you.

Actions that showed love & respect

_____
_____
_____

Moments that gave mixed signals

_____
_____
_____

Actions that clearly hurt or disrespected

_____
_____
_____

God's truth shows me what to stop, pause, or keep moving toward.

Fantasy vs. Truth Table

On the left, write the "fantasies" or false hopes (e.g., "She'll come back"). On the right, write the "truths" God revealed

(e.g., "She told me to let go").

Fantasies	Truths

The truth may sting, but it is
also what sets me free.

Guard Your Heart Plan

On each ray, write a boundary you'll keep to protect your heart (ex: Not chasing, Not ignoring God's signs, Not begging for love).

My
Peace

Above all else, guard your heart.

-Proverbs 4:23

Release & Redirect Ritual

What I release...

Write names,hopes,or false beliefs you need to let go

_____

_____

_____

Where I redirect my energy...

Write where you will now pour that love (God, career,
purpose, self-care, dreams)

_____

_____

_____

_____

Rcleasing them is making room for
God's blessing.

Voices I follow

Circle 1:Voices I listened to(psychics,friends,fears,desires). God's voice (truth, scripture, peace). Middle: write what happens when the two conflict.

Voices I listened to

psychics, friends, fears, desires

_____

_____

God's voice

truth, scripture, peace

_____

_____

When the two conflict...

_____

_____

_____

_____

God is not author of confusion.
- 1 Corinthians 14:33

Letter of Closure

Write a letter (you will not send) to the person who ghosted you: Start with: "I release you because..." End with: "I trust God's plan for me more than I desire your presence."

_____

_____

_____

_____

_____

_____

_____

_____

_____

_____

_____

_____

_____

_____

Closure is not found in their words, but in God's truth.

Chapter 3: Introspecting

After walking through the heartbreak and fantasy of love that wasn't real, I had to stop and face something harder — myself. Introspection isn't easy. It requires peeling back layers and asking: Why do I love the way I do? Why do I hold on so tightly? Why do I give even when it costs me?

At just two years old, I didn't have a father around. That absence planted a seed of abandonment that grew silently inside me. Even as I got older, I didn't say it out loud, but it whispered in the background: don't let people leave, don't let people go. That feeling deepened when my cousins — the ones I laughed with, played with, and built my childhood around — moved away. I still remember watching boxes being packed, hearing the grown-ups talk about 'new beginnings,' and not fully understanding why their leaving had to mean my world would suddenly feel smaller.

When they were gone, the silence was deafening. The rooms that once echoed with laughter felt empty, and I felt empty too. I didn't have words for it then, but it was as if a part of my safety net had been cut away. I wasn't looking to be seen — I just wanted to feel secure, wanted to know the people I loved would always be nearby. But instead, I was left with an ache I couldn't name, a loneliness that wrapped itself around me and reminded me how much it hurt when people I loved weren't there. That wound stayed with me, quietly shaping the way I held on to connections later in life — not because I thought love was temporary, but because I never wanted to feel that kind of loneliness again.

The one constant I had was my brother. To me, he wasn't just a sibling — he was my hero. Ten years older, he was the steady presence I could count on, a friend, a protector, and the closest thing I had to a father figure. He was patient with me, teaching me how to play basketball, how to take the shot even when I missed, and how to keep going when the game got tough. He let me tag along on his flag football teams, never making me feel like I didn't belong, and we spent countless hours lost in video games together.

Those moments weren't just memories — they were lifelines. They gave me joy, comfort, and a sense of belonging I craved so deeply. To this day, they are etched in my heart as some of the purest times of my childhood. But as I grew, so did he. Because of our age gap, life naturally pulled him into his own path — building his own family, stepping fully into manhood. I was proud of him, inspired by him, yet when that season shifted, I felt another wave of loneliness wash over me. It was never his fault — it was simply life moving forward. Still, his absence left a mark, because he had been more than just my brother. He was my role model, my safe place, and the one who showed me what love, and guidance could look like.

My mom has always been my superhero. To this day, she still calls me her sidekick and best friend—but the truth is, I've admired her far more than I ever knew how to express. Her faith, her prayer life, and her unshakable relationship with God carried me and my brother through seasons we might not have survived without her. I watched her stand tall in moments that would have broken most people, and in my eyes, she became the definition of resilience, courage, and unconditional love.

I also saw how deeply she loved others—how she gave without boundaries, always pouring out her heart to help and uplift those around her. Watching her carry so much on her own left a quiet imprint on me. It taught me, without words, that strength meant handling everything yourself, never asking for help, and always holding it all together no matter what it cost.

Eventually, I took that belief into my relationships. Because I loved so deeply, my care sometimes showed up as control. I thought protecting, fixing, and holding on tightly was the way you proved your love. I didn't realize I was repeating what I had seen: one person doing the emotional lifting for everyone else.

Now, I'm learning that love with boundaries is still love, and maybe an even stronger form of it. I'm discovering that vulnerability isn't weakness and that God never intended for one heart to hold the weight of an entire world. Setting healthy boundaries is its own form of strength and a new way to love.

What I didn't understand back then was that true love and true strength don't come from control — they come from trust. God had to reteach me that the weight I was carrying was never mine to bear alone. He reminded me of His word: "Trust in the Lord with all your heart and lean not on your own understanding; in all your ways submit to Him, and He will make your paths straight" (Proverbs 3:5–6). Watching my mom shaped me, but it was God who showed me that my strength was not in doing it all by myself, but in surrendering to Him."

The truth is no one can stand alone forever.
From ages 18 to 23, me and my mom were homeless, moving place to place, living with family and friends. That season broke us but also built us. The crazy thing? In our hardest times, we realized we were living out the very prayers we prayed. We had asked God to restore relationships with loved ones, and while we didn't have a stable home, we ended up with the very people we prayed to be closer to. In the end, God restored a roof over our heads — showing us that even in the storm, He was faithful.

As I grew older, I slowly started to build some kind of bond with my father. It's not perfect, but it's something. And I trust God is still writing that story.

Looking back, I see the roots: abandonment, loneliness, resilience, survival. I also see how those roots shaped how I loved — why I clung to people, why I gave too much, why I struggled to put myself first. And just as much, I see how silence became my shield. When people made fun of me, I swallowed every word I wanted to say. I kept my mouth shut, not because I didn't feel the pain, but because I was afraid of what might come out if I let it loose. My silence wasn't peace — it was survival. Every laugh I ignored, every cruel word I let slide, stacked inside me like bricks, building a wall I thought would keep me safe. Behind that wall, my inner child carried the wounds of rejection, and my shadow self-held the fire of everything I never said.

Now, in adulthood, I find myself finally speaking those words — the ones I should have spoken long ago. They come heavy, trembling, but they come out. And the difference is, I'm not afraid of my voice anymore. I claim it, I honor it, and I use it to stand strong in ways that little girl never could. Introspection opened my eyes to the fact that my past wasn't just in my past — it was alive in my patterns. And God was showing me it was time to face it.

Your Turn to Reflect

Scriptures to Meditate On
"The Lord is close to the brokenhearted and saves those who are crushed in spirit." – Psalm 34:18

"I will not leave you as orphans; I will come to you." – John 14:18
"Cast all your anxiety on Him because He cares for you." – 1 Peter 5:7

Reflection Questions

What childhood experiences shaped how you see love and abandonment?

_____
_____
_____
_____
_____

Who were the people that stood in the gap for you, like my brother did for me — and how did their presence impact your life?

_____
_____
_____
_____
_____

In what ways have you carried old wounds into current or past relationships?

_____

_____

_____

_____

_____

Where do you still struggle with putting yourself first, and how could that change your healing journey?

_____

_____

_____

_____

_____

How has God shown you His presence in times of loneliness or instability?

_____

_____

_____

_____

Closing Prayer

Heavenly Father,

Thank You for never abandoning me, even in moments when I felt alone. Help me see the roots of my wounds clearly so I can surrender them to You. Heal the places in me that still fear rejection, and remind me daily that I am chosen, loved, and secure in You. Give me courage to put myself first in a way that honors You and protects the heart You've given me. Surround me with people who reflect Your love and remind me that I never walk alone.

In Jesus' name, Amen.

CHAPTER THREE
Root Mapping Exercise

On each root write a boundary you'll keep to protect your heart (ex: Not chasing, Not ignoring God's signs, Not begging for love).

The root explains the fruit. With God, roots can be healed.

Inner Child Dialogue

In the adult's bubble: Write your response
today(ex:"You are safe now. God will never leave
you.").

Reflect: What did your inner child need most that
you can give yourself today?

_____

_____

_____

_____

Speak to your younger self with
the love you needed then.

Silence vs. Love

Think of moments you stayed silent when you were hurt,
and write them below. Then, write what you wish
you had said or what you can say now.

Moments I stayed silent	What I wish I had said

Reflect:

How has silence been your shield?

How will your voice now become your strength?

Your silence kept you safe. Your voice will set you free.

Lonliness Inventory

Write down 3-5 moments when you felt most
alone.
Next to each moment, write how God showed up
(through people, prayer, or resilience). Finish with
the sentence: "Even in my emptiness, God filled
me with ...

When I felt alone   How God showed up

_____   _____

_____   _____

_____   _____

_____   _____

_____   _____

_____   _____

Even in my empitness, God filled me with ...

_____

_____

_____

Never will I leave you; never will I forsake you." –
Hebrews 13:5

Resilience Timeline

Mark key ages/seasons (childhood, teenage years, homelessness season, adulthood). Under each, write 1 wound you carried and 1 strength it gave you. At the end of the timeline, write: "My resilience isn't from me — it's from God's hand on my life."

Childhood	Teenage Years	Homelessness Season

_____

_____

1 wound   Strength

_____

_____

What broke you also built you.

What I Release To God

Burdens

_____

_____

_____

_____

Prayer of Surrender

Lord, I release _____ into Your hands.

_____

_____

_____

I trust You to heal what I cannot carry alone.

_____

_____

"Trust in the Lord with all your heart." - Proverbs 3:5

Chapter 4: When God Speaks in Unexpected Ways
(Psychic Readings, Inner Child, and Shadow Healing)

I never thought I would be the type of person to watch psychic readings. I wasn't someone who picked up the Bible and just read it cover to cover, and honestly, at that time in my life, I wasn't even looking for God in the places He usually shows up. But God knows His children. He knows what will capture our attention, what will hold us long enough for Him to slip truth into our hearts. For me, it was those readings.

At first, I thought it was all about love — about figuring out this "twin flame" connection I believed I had found. I was hungry for answers, desperate for clarity. But what I didn't realize at the time was that God was using my desire for understanding as a doorway to Himself.

The readings began to reveal things I couldn't see on my own. They pointed out that black magic was at play in my life — not just from my karmic ex, but also from others who were jealous, bitter, or secretly hoping for my downfall. At first, I couldn't believe it. But as the patterns unfolded, I realized God was opening my eyes to what spiritual warfare really looks like.

Many people hear "black magic" and think of candles, altars, or spells. But it's deeper than that. Black magic is any dark intention meant to harm another. It can look like malicious thoughts, gossip and slander, wishing harm on someone, withholding blessings out of envy, using someone's personal items with ill intent, energy vampirism, harboring resentment, or even the evil eye. These things might not leave visible scars, but they are very real in the spiritual world.

When I started watching the readings, I got a better understanding of what dark witches and white witches were. A lot of religious people would be against psychics, but it really depends on what psychic — or what forces — you're listening to or allowing into your life. No, I do not practice the rituals psychics may do. But watching them made me realize that even in religion and Christianity, we also practice rituals. Praying, using blessing oil, fasting, meditation, Scripture reading, journaling, funerals, communion, worship services, singing or chanting, speaking in tongues, baptism, offerings, and even weddings — all of these are ritual practices too.

Even God Himself used signs in creation to guide His people. The wise men followed a star to find the Messiah (Matthew 2:2, 9–10). And Genesis tells us, "Let there be lights in the expanse of the heavens to separate the day from the night. And let them be for signs and for seasons, and for days and years" (Genesis 1:14). God has always spoken through the heavens and through nature.

The readings also helped me get a better understanding of what me and my twin flame were going through. It wasn't just about me healing; she had her own internal healing to do. She ghosted me not because she didn't care, but because she didn't feel worthy of me. I remember her saying those words: that I deserved more. As painful as that was, hearing confirmation of it through the readings showed me that God was talking to me, leading me, and reminding me that this journey was part of a bigger plan.

The readings showed me that this darkness was interfering not only with my twin flame journey, but with my own peace, clarity, and strength. And yet, instead of leaving me fearful, God used it to teach me. He opened my eyes to the reality of spiritual warfare — that "we wrestle not against flesh and blood, but against principalities, against powers, against the rulers of the darkness of this world, against spiritual wickedness in high places" (Ephesians 6:12).

This revelation shifted everything. Instead of being consumed with what my karmic ex was doing or how people felt about me, I started to look higher. I began to see that I didn't need to fight back with the same weapons. My strength was in prayer, in worship, in guarding my spirit. God reminded me that "no weapon formed against you shall prosper, and every tongue that rises against you in judgment you shall condemn" (Isaiah 54:17).

Even when others plotted against me, He covered me. Even when people spoke curses, He declared blessing. What the enemy meant for harm, God was using for my growth. And slowly, I began to see that spiritual warfare wasn't about fear — it was about learning to walk in the authority God had already given me. And as for my twin flame — I don't see her presence in my life as something meant to harm me intentionally. Yes, what happened between us hurt deeply, but I now understand it differently. She was a blessing in disguise — a mirror reflecting the shadow parts of myself that I needed to face. She became the catalyst for my spiritual awakening. Even the black magic that came against me only fueled my determination to grow, to heal, and to strengthen myself both as a person and spiritually.

But it wasn't just her reflecting things back to me — I was reflecting on her as well. I led with my heart, which is my feminine energy, while she led with logic, which was her masculine energy. Where I was showing her love and vulnerability, she was wrestling with walls built from her past pain. I was teaching her, in my own way, how to open up again, how to love freely, and how to allow herself to be vulnerable. Just as she mirrored my shadows back to me, I was showing her the parts of herself that longed to heal but were afraid to trust.

It was in this space — in the middle of learning about inner child healing, shadow work, and spiritual warfare — that I started to truly understand God's presence in my life. He wasn't distant. He was right there, teaching me through every layer, breaking illusions, and preparing me to rise stronger than ever.

Reflection: God's Protection in Spiritual Warfare

When God opened my eyes to black magic and spiritual warfare, I realized the fight was never truly against people. It wasn't about my karmic ex, jealous friends, or even strangers who wished harm. It was about the unseen battle for my soul, my peace, and my destiny.

The enemy may use people, but God uses truth. And His truth always sets us free.

Reflection Questions:

What areas of your life feel weighed down by invisible battles?

_____
_____
_____
_____
_____
_____

Are you carrying wounds that come from gossip, rejection, or envy from others?

_____
_____
_____
_____

How have you seen God protect you in ways you didn't understand at the time?

_____
_____
_____
_____

Are you willing to trust His covering even when you can't see the whole picture?

_____
_____
_____
_____
_____

Remember: You are not powerless. You are armed with faith, prayer, and God's promises.
"The Lord will fight for you; you need only to be still." – Exodus 14:14

"No weapon formed against you shall prosper, and every tongue which rises against you in judgment you shall condemn. This is the heritage of the servants of the Lord, and their righteousness is from Me," says the Lord. – Isaiah 54:17

Closing Prayer: Covering in Spiritual Warfare

Heavenly Father,

Thank You for opening my eyes to the truth of spiritual warfare. Thank You for showing me that no weapon formed against me shall prosper (Isaiah 54:17), and that greater is He who is in me than he who is in the world (1 John 4:4).

I ask You now to guard my heart, my mind, and my spirit. Break every chain of fear, rejection, envy, or bitterness that has tried to attach itself to me. Remove every curse, every word of harm, every thought of evil spoken against me, and replace it with Your blessing.
Lord, help me to walk in the authority You've given me. Remind me daily that I am covered by the blood of Jesus, that angels encamp around those who fear Him, and He delivers them (Psalm 34:7), and that Your Spirit lives within me. Give me discernment to recognize when the enemy is at work, and the strength to stand firm in Your truth.

Father, let my life be a testimony of Your protection and power. And may every battle I face only bring me closer to You.

In Jesus' name, Amen.

Unexpected Signs Tracker

Write about 3-5 moments when God spoke to you in an unexpected way (dreams, a reading, a stranger's words, a song, nature, etc.). For each moment, ask:

- What did I notice?
- How did it make me feel?
- What truth was God showing me through it?

Moment 1

What did I notice?

_____

_____

How did it make me feel?

_____

_____

Moment 2

What did I notice?

_____

_____

How did it make me feel?

_____

_____

Moment 5

What did I notice?

_____

_____

How did it make me feel?

_____

_____

Moment 4

What did I notice?

_____

_____

What truth was God
showing me through it?

_____

_____

God's voice may surprise you, but it will always
lead you to peace.

Identifying Spiritual Warfare

Reflect on the ways a spiritual attack has threatened you and how God protected you through it.

Dark Intentions I've Faced	God's Protection Over Me

"No weapon formed against me shall prosper." – Isaiah 54:17

Shadow Self Mirror

Inside the mirror, list traits or wounds you see reflected back in others (jealousy, fear of abandonment, control, alls in love). Next to each, write: "What this mirror taught me about myself.....

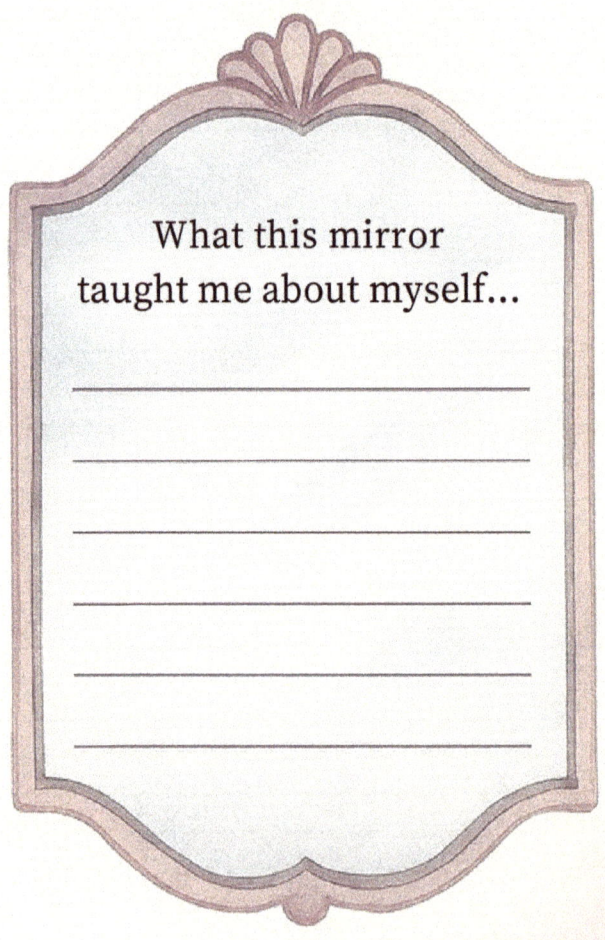

What this mirror
taught me about myself...

_____

_____

_____

_____

_____

_____

My shadow does not define me-
it refines me.

Inner Child Healing Letter

Write a letter to your inner child, starting with:

"I see you. I know you felt.———.   But now I want you
to know..."

Include affirmations like: "You are safe now. You are loved.
You do not need to beg to be chosen."
End the letter with a prayer asking God to cover that
younger version of you with healing.

**The child within you
deserves to feel safe.**

Twin Flame Reflection Map

What she mirrored in me shadows, insecuritties, wounds exposed

_____

_____

_____

_____

_____

What I mirrored in her strengths, love, vulnerability you reflected back

_____

_____

_____

_____

This connection was not to break me, but to awaken me.

Authority In Christ Declaration

Write down 5 lies the enemy has spoken over your life.
Next to each, write the Scripture truth that destroys it.

Lie	Scripture Truth
1	
2	
3	
4	
5	

By the authority of Christ, I walk in...

We wrestle not against flesh and blood...
- Ephesians 6:12

Chapter 5: Inner Child & Shadow Self-Healing

When God began to open my eyes to spiritual warfare, I realized something: not every battle is outside of me. Some of the hardest battles were inside — in the hidden places of my own heart.

The psychic readings had revealed black magic at play, but God revealed something deeper. Yes, there were people sending negativity, curses, and envied my way. Yes, the enemy tried to interfere with my twin flame journey. But God showed me the greatest fight wasn't only against outside forces — it was against the broken pieces of me that still believed lies about myself.

That's when I was introduced to the concepts of the inner child and the shadow self. At first, I didn't even understand what those words meant. But slowly, God began to teach me. And if I'm honest, a lot of that understanding came after watching readings that confirmed what I was feeling but couldn't yet name. Those moments became the flashlight that shined into corners I hadn't wanted to face.

The inner child is that part of me that still carries the voice of a little girl — the one who longed for a father who wasn't there, who struggled when cousins moved away, who felt alone even when surrounded by people. She was the one who wanted so badly to hold on to love, even if it was toxic, because the thought of abandonment was more painful than the reality of rejection.

At just two years old, I didn't have a father around, and that absence planted a seed of abandonment that grew quietly inside me. My inner child felt it even when I couldn't put words to it — that whisper in the background saying: don't let people leave, don't let people go.

I began to heal by finally acknowledging that absence instead of pretending it didn't affect me. God reminded me that He was the Father who never left. I prayed over that wound and started to re-parent myself — telling that little girl, "You weren't left because you were unworthy. You are chosen. You are loved."

When my cousins moved away, that whisper grew louder. They were my playmates, my laughter, my safety net — and watching them leave felt like my world was shrinking. I didn't understand why people had to go, and all I knew was that it left me feeling small and powerless.

I honored that memory by letting myself grieve it as an adult instead of brushing it off. I realized the ache wasn't a weakness — it was proof of how deeply I loved it. Part of my healing came by allowing myself to form new connections, but this time with healthy boundaries, knowing I could survive loss without losing myself.

My brother became my safe place. To the little girl in me, he was more than a brother — he was protection, belonging, the steady presence I could cling to. But when life pulled him into his own world, that familiar emptiness came rushing back. It wasn't his fault, but my inner child felt the loss all over again.

I healed by reframing the story: his leaving wasn't rejection — it was life. Instead of seeing it as another loss, I chose to carry his lessons with me — basketball, perseverance, laughter — as gifts he planted in me that could never be taken away.

And then there was my mom — strong, resilient, unshakable. She carried everything like a superhero, but what I didn't realize then was how much her strength imprinted on me. My shadow learned to stay quiet, to never ask for help, to believe that holding it all in was the only way to survive.

God showed me that strength isn't silence or control, it's surrender. I began to heal by unlearning the lie that I had to carry everything myself. Prayer, community, and learning to ask for help became part of rewriting that script.

My inner child carried all these experiences: abandonment, loneliness, survival mode, the desire to be loved without conditions. She lived in me, quietly shaping the choices I made as an adult.

Then came the shadow self.

The shadow is the side we don't want to admit exists. For me, it was the anger that rose up when I was betrayed. The bitterness that wanted to take root when people left. The exhaustion that made me shut down when life became too heavy. It was the part of me that wanted to hide my pain instead of exposing it.

But God didn't show me my shadow so I could shame it or bury it deeper. He showed me so I could bring it into the light. Healing doesn't come from pretending everything is okay. Healing comes from honesty — from saying, yes, I am hurt, yes, I am angry, yes, I feel abandoned — but I am still here, and God is still with me. Silence became my shield. When people laughed at me or made jokes at my expense, I swallowed every word that rose in my throat. I kept my mouth shut, not because the pain wasn't real, but because I was afraid of what would come out if I let it loose. My silence wasn't peace — it was armor. Each laugh I ignored, each cruel word I let slide, stack up like bricks, and behind those bricks I hid the most fragile parts of myself.

My inner child lived behind that wall, carrying the wounds of rejection, longing for someone to defend her, aching to be seen and protected. She felt powerless, small, and unseen — yet she learned how to survive by pretending their words didn't matter, by walking away when all she really wanted to do was cry or scream. That silence was her way of surviving.

I healed by finally letting my voice rise. Speaking my truth in adulthood — even when my voice trembled — became a spiritual act. Each time I said "no," told my story, or refused to minimize my pain, I dismantled a brick from that wall.

My shadow self-lived there too, holding the fire of everything I never said. She was rage disguised as composure. She was the part of me that wanted to fight back, to throw every cruel word back in their faces. But fear chained her down — fear that if she spoke, she'd be punished, ridiculed, or abandoned even more. So, she stayed hidden, her power locked away, her fire smoldering in the dark.

I healed by giving that fire a safe outlet. Journaling, prayer, and naming my anger out loud allowed me to release it without destruction. Over time, I reclaimed that rage not as shame but as strength — fire that could be used to protect, not to destroy.

That was the war inside me: the wounded child who swallowed her pain, and the shadow self who held the anger like a secret flame.

And yet — even flames hidden in the dark don't die. They wait. Now, as a woman, I can finally let that fire rise. My words may tremble, but they come out. My voice no longer feels dangerous — it feels holy. It is the voice of the child who longed for safety and the shadow who carried my power.

I healed by realizing that my worth isn't tied to who stays or leaves. God's presence gave me the courage to speak even when people didn't agree or applaud. Every time I used my voice and stood firm in my truth, I broke another chain of fear.

But part of that healing also came when I remembered my name — Shechinahglory, which means God's Presence. My very name was a reminder that I was never abandoned, never forgotten, never alone. Even in rejection, His presence was with me. Speaking my truth was no longer about earning approval — it was about walking in the identity God gave me from the beginning.

Together, they remind me: I am no longer silenced. I am no longer hiding. I am whole.

Reflection: Meeting Your Inner Child and Shadow

Healing doesn't mean erasing your past. It means seeing the little girl (or boy) inside of you who still remembers the moments of pain, loneliness, and survival — and choosing to love them fully. It means naming the anger, grief, or fear that hides in the shadow, and inviting God's light to touch those places.

When you honor your inner child and bring your shadow into the light, you break the chains of silence. You step out of survival mode and into wholeness.

How It All Connects

Think of it this way:

Introspection → The flashlight. It helps you see what's inside.

Inner Child Work → You discover the wounded child inside the room.

Shadow Work → You see the hidden, darker corners where rejected parts live.

More Introspection → You keep reflecting to understand, heal, and bring those pieces back into wholeness.

Introspection is both the beginning and the continuing process. Without it, you can't really meet your inner child or shadow self. But after meeting them, you keep introspecting to integrate the lessons and healing.

Scriptures for Guidance

Psalm 34:18 — "The Lord is close to the brokenhearted and saves those who are crushed in spirit."

Isaiah 41:10 — "So do not fear, for I am with you; do not be dismayed, for I am your God. I will strengthen you and help you; I will uphold you with my righteous right hand."

Ephesians 5:13 — "But everything exposed by the light becomes visible—and everything that is illuminated becomes a light."

2 Corinthians 12:9 — "My grace is sufficient for you, for my power is made perfect in weakness."

Reflection Questions

When you think of your younger self, what memory or image comes to mind first?

_____

_____

_____

_____

What hidden emotions or "shadow" traits do you often try to push away?

_____

_____

_____

_____

How has your past shaped the way you give or receive love today?

_____

_____

_____

_____

What would you say to your inner child if you could sit with them right now?

_____

_____

_____

_____

_____

_____

_____

_____

Where do you see God's hand even in the moments that once felt like abandonment?

_____

_____

_____

_____

Closing Prayer

Heavenly Father,

I bring my inner child before You — the part of me that still remembers what it felt like to be unseen, unloved, or left behind. I ask that You hold them in Your arms, that You remind them they are safe, cherished, and never alone.

I bring my shadow before You — the parts of me I've tried to hide, the anger, the grief, the pain. Instead of shame, cover me with Your grace. Instead of hiding, teach me to surrender these places to Your light.

Lord, help me to walk in wholeness. Teach me that my worth is not defined by who left, but by You — the One who has never abandoned me. Heal what was broken, restore what was lost, and remind me daily that Your love is enough.

In Jesus' name, Amen.

Meeting Your Inner Child

1. Close your eyes and imagine yourself as a child (age 2-7). 2. Ask: "What did she/he/they need most in that moment?

3. Write a dialogue:
Inner Child: "I feel.."

_____

_____

_____

Adult You: "I want you to know..."

_____

_____

_____

I am here for you now. You are safe. You are loved.

_____

_____

God places the lonely in families. - Psalm 68:6

Shadow Self Reflection

Write down 3 traits or emotions you hide (anger, jealousy, bitterness, fear, shame).

_____

_____

_____

_____

1. When does this show up?

_____

2. What is it protecting me from?

_____

3. How can I bring it into God's light.

_____

_____

"The light shines in the darkness, and the darkness has not overcome it." – John 1:5

Letter Of Representing

Write a letter beginning: "Dear Little Me, I see you. I know you felt __. But now I want you to know…" Tell your inner child what you wish someone had told you when you felt abandoned, overlooked, or silenced. Close with: "God is your forever Father. You are chosen, you are whole."

_____

_____

_____

_____

_____

_____

_____

_____

_____

God is your forever Father. You are chosen, you are loved.

Safe Anger Release

Make two lists:

Unspoken Words I've Held In	How I Can Release Them Safely
_____	_____
_____	_____
_____	_____
_____	_____
_____	_____

Write out one thing you've wanted to scream but never said— then reframe it as a declaration of strength.

Example: Instead of "You hurt me!"
→ "I will not let others define my worth again.

_____

_____

Be angry, and do not sin...
Ephesians 4:26

Breaking The Silence Wall

On each 'brick,' write one lie or fear that kept you silent. Underneath, write God's truth that smashes the brick.

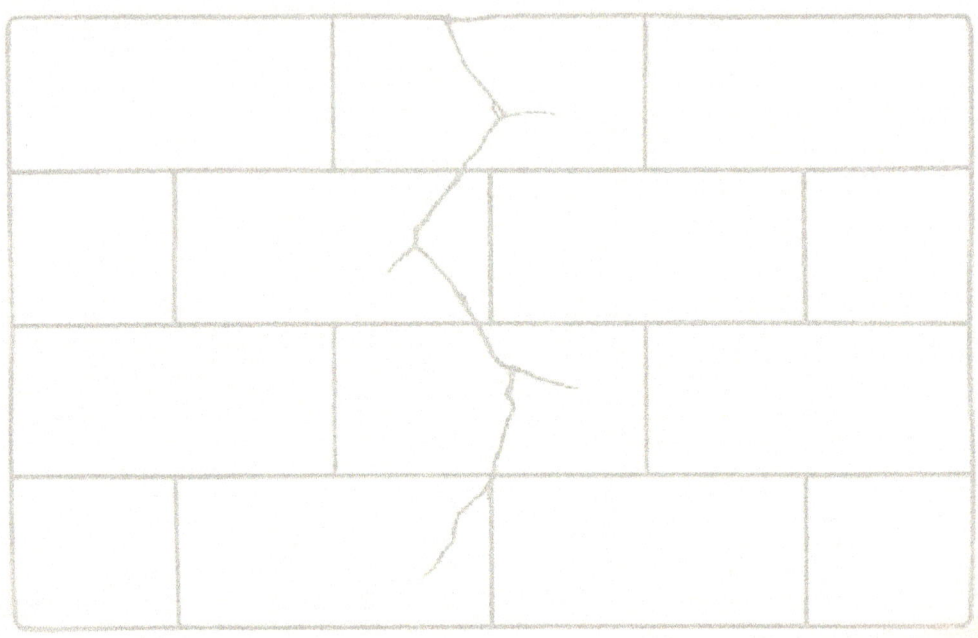

Once complete, draw or write how your voice feels when it is free.

"The truth will set me free." – John 8:32

Name & Identity Meditation

1. Write your name (first, middle, or full).

2. Research or meditate on what it means.

3. Answer:

   What does my name remind me about who I am?
   How does God's presence show up in my identity?

4. Create a personal mantra beginning with your name:

Shechinahglory
-I am never abandoned. God's
presence goes with me.

My Name (and meaning)

What my name reminds me about who I am

How God's presence shows up in my identity

My personal mantra

God's presence defines my identity.

Chapter 6: Vision Between Worlds
Dreams as Spiritual Messages

I didn't ask for the dreams to come, they just did. Some were so vivid they felt more real than my waking life. I'd wake up sweating, with tears on my face, or carrying a heaviness I couldn't shake for days. Back then, I didn't fully understand them. But now I know: those dreams were God's way of showing me truths I wasn't ready to face in the natural world.

I dreamed of people who meant harm to me before I discovered their intentions in real life. I dreamed of storms that mirrored the chaos in my relationships. I dreamed of houses — some broken down, only to realize they represented me, my heart, and my soul. What I thought was just random images turned out to be spiritual revelations. God was opening my eyes through visions at night. Just as He used psychic readings to expose the reality of spiritual warfare, He used my dreams to make it personal. It was His way of whispering, "Pay attention, I'm speaking."

There are places I've traveled to that my feet have never touched. There are conversations I've had with souls who never stood before me in the waking world.
And there are moments so vivid, so urgent, they felt less like dreams and more like warnings carved into the fabric of my spirit. Dreams are not just images; they are messages. They are the quiet voice of the soul, speaking in symbols, colors, and impossible scenes that carry meaning far beyond the surface. In this realm between sleep and waking, I have been a witness, a traveler, and sometimes a rescuer in battles only my spirit could fight.

These visions are not random. They are threads of the unseen— connecting my spirit to people, places, and truths I could never have known otherwise. They taught me to listen with my heart, to pay attention, and to treat the dream world as a sacred space where God, my higher self, and my ancestors could reach me without the noise of the day.

This was only the beginning of how God trained me to see beyond the surface.

What follows are not just stories of the night, but lessons etched into my soul. Each dream is a doorway, and on the other side, there is always something waiting to be revealed.

The Road That Disappeared:

The night was thick with silence, broken only by the low hum of my 18-wheeler. My hands were steady on the wheel, my eyes fixed ahead as the truck rolled through the dark stretch of highway. The headlights cut through the blackness, and even the streetlights above glowed a dull, tired yellow. The road felt endless, but it was familiar — a space I knew how to navigate.

And then, without warning, everything shifted.

The truck began to slow. My foot pressed harder on the accelerator, but it was like the machine had decided on its own pace. The headlights blinked out. The streetlights, too. Darkness swallowed everything in front of me, thick and absolute.

I could no longer see the road directly ahead — just a void where asphalt should have been. But in the distance, far ahead, a faint, hazy light shimmered. It was small, almost mocking, as if it knew how far away it was. Something in me believed that if I just kept going, I would reach it.

The truck groaned forward, each movement heavier than the last. My vision stayed locked on that distant glow, but my gut twisted with unease. I didn't see the danger until it was too late.

The ground beneath me gave way.

First a lurch.

Then a pull.

Then the sickening realization: I was sinking.

The cab of the 18-wheeler tilted forward as if bowing to the earth, its weight dragging me down into a pit of quicksand. The tires disappeared beneath a slow, greedy wave of dirt and sludge. My breath caught in my throat. Panic bloomed in my chest like fire.

Frantically, I clawed at the door handle, searching for a way out. My hands shook as I reached for my phone — my one lifeline. My heart slammed in my ears, each beat louder than the last, as the truck sank deeper, swallowing the dash, the windshield, the air.

And then... nothing; I was awake.

Reflection:

When I woke, my heart was still racing. I could feel the phantom heaviness of the sinking truck, the helplessness of being trapped inside it. I've had enough dreams to know they don't always speak plain language. This one felt like a warning — about false light, about pushing toward something that looks like salvation but leaves you blind to what's directly in front of you.

The slow crawl toward that distant glow reminded me of times I've chased goals or relationships that seemed promising, only to realize I was losing myself along the way. The quicksand was the weight of my own doubt, fear, and exhaustion — swallowing me whole when I ignored the signs to stop and reevaluate my path.

This dream told me: Not every light is meant to be followed.

Symbolic Breakdown

- The 18-Wheeler → Represents my life's journey and responsibilities. Driving something so large means I carry a heavy load — my past, my ambitions, my commitments. In spiritual dreams, a truck often symbolizes how much we are carrying emotionally and mentally.

- The Sudden Darkness → A moment of uncertainty or confusion in life. Losing all light at once suggests a loss of clarity, guidance, or faith.

- The Distant Glow → False hope, distractions, or illusions. Sometimes we see a glimmer far ahead and believe it will save us, but it's not always divine guidance — it can be temptation or misdirection.

- The Quicksand → Hidden dangers or emotional traps. In shadow work, this can represent unresolved trauma or patterns that pull us down when we're not grounded.

- The Phone in My Hand → My ability to call for help — a reminder that even in moments of sinking, I have the means to reach out and not suffer in silence.

Integration Exercise *(extra journal pages 111-112pg)*

Recall a Time You Chased Something Far Away. Think of a situation where you were so focused on a distant goal, relationship, or dream that you overlooked what was happening in the present moment.

_____
_____
_____
_____
_____

Identify the Signs You Ignored. Write down at least three red flags, gut feelings, or warnings you noticed but chose not to act on.

_____
_____
_____
_____
_____

Recognize the "False Light". Describe what drew you toward it. Was it beauty, promise, escape, validation?

_____
_____
_____
_____
_____
_____
_____

Ground Yourself in the Present. Write one paragraph about something good and solid in your life right now that deserves more of your attention.

_____
_____
_____
_____
_____

Affirm Your Direction

End with this affirmation:

"I will not chase illusions. I honor the light that is real and close, and I trust the steps God has set before me."

Spiritual Protection Notes

1. Pray for Clear Direction

   o "I will not chase false light. My steps are ordered and protected."

2. Read Your Bible

   o Psalm 119:105 (God's word as a lamp), Isaiah 30:21 (hearing God's direction).

3. Cleanse the Energy of Your Route (Symbolic Act)

   o Anoint your car or shoes with oil before traveling.

4. Cleanse Your Mind

   o Journaling before bed to release confusion and anxiety.

5. Visualize the True Light

   o In prayer, picture the light of God ahead of you, removing all shadows.

6. Close the Gate

"I will not be led into traps or darkness. My journey is covered by divine light."

The Mirror on the Road:

The road was the same as before — two narrow lanes slicing through a forest so dense it swallowed the moonlight. The trees pressed in like silent witnesses, their shadows bending over the asphalt. I was in my 18-wheeler again, its engine a steady hum beneath me. The headlights reached out into the darkness, and far ahead, a single faint light glowed at the end of the road.

The air felt heavier this time. The darkness wasn't just around me — it was inside the truck, pressing against my skin.

The more I drove toward the glow, the more the road seemed to stretch. What should have been a few minutes of driving felt endless, as if the road itself was trying to keep me away. My truck slowed without my doing, the pedal under my foot stiff and unresponsive.

And then I saw it — saw her.

On the opposite lane, heading in the other direction, was another person standing there looking at me... me standing there looking at me.

Outside the cab, through the glass, I saw me. Same locs, same clothes, same expression — except she wasn't looking at the road. She was looking at me. Our eyes locked for what felt like hours, my reflection moving forward as I sat frozen.

The darkness around me thickened. My lights were on, but they didn't reach the road ahead. The glow at the far end was still there, still fainting, but I couldn't tell if it was calling me closer or warning me away.

Then the other me was gone — swallowed by the black. My truck sat stranded in the middle of the road, unmoving, as the silence pressed in like a weight. Fear wrapped around my chest until I couldn't breathe. And then...

I woke up.

Reflection

This dream didn't carry the chaos of sinking into quicksand, but it carried something deeper — a mirror I didn't ask to investigate. Seeing myself standing in the opposite direction of the road, I felt like watching a version of me I couldn't reach, as if she was living a life parallel to mine but on a completely different path.

It left me with questions:

Am I chasing the wrong light?

Is there another version of me who made different choices?

Or is she a warning — the me I become if I keep going the way I am?

The stranded feeling, stuck in the dark between where I was and where I thought I needed to go, mirrored real-life moments where I felt caught between moving forward and turning back.

Symbolic Breakdown

- The 18-Wheeler → Life's journey and the weight of my responsibilities.

- The Stretched Road → Delayed progress; goals that keep feeling further away the more I try to reach them.

- The Other Me → Shadow self, alternate timeline, or unacknowledged parts of my identity.

- The Glow at the End → Ambition or hope, but possibly a distraction from what's right in front of me.

- The Darkness → The unknown; fears and unresolved issues that block clarity.

- Being Stranded → Feeling powerless or directionless in waking life.

Integration Exercise

Think of a time you felt "stuck" between two versions of yourself
— the person you are now and the person you could be if you
made a different choice. Which direction felt safer? Which
direction felt truer? What fears held you in place?

_____
_____
_____
_____
_____
_____
_____

Reflect on a Time You Saw Two Possible Versions of Yourself.
Think of a moment when you felt torn between who you are now
and who you could become if you made a different choice.

_____
_____
_____
_____
_____

Describe Each Version Honestly. Write one paragraph about the
"you" that stayed on the current path.

_____
_____
_____
_____
_____

Write another about the "you" who might have taken the other
road.

_____
_____
_____
_____
_____

Look for the Warning Signs. Did either version of you feel false, disconnected, or misaligned with your spirit? Write down what made you feel that way.

_____
_____
_____
_____
_____
_____

Reconnect With Your True Self. Write one action you can take right now to strengthen your connection to the path that feels authentic to you.

_____
_____
_____
_____
_____

Affirm Your Alignment

"I walk the road that belongs to me. I trust the path God has lit for my life, and I release all false versions of myself."

Spiritual Protection Notes

1. Pray for Discernment of Self

   o "I see myself through the eyes of truth, not deception. I walk the path God has set for me."

2. Read Your Bible

   o Proverbs 3:5-6 (guidance), James 1:5 (wisdom).

3. Cleanse Your Path (Symbolic Act)

- Sweep your front walkway or driveway while praying for clarity in your journey.

4. Cleanse Your Spirit

   - Burn frankincense or myrrh for purification and clear vision.

5. Visualize Merging with Your True Self

   - See yourself stepping fully into the version God has called you to be.

6. Close the Gate

   - "No false reflection may lead me astray. My path is illuminated by truth."

The Whisper in the Dark

I was asleep, my body was heavy and still. The room was quiet, the air thick.

Then I felt a weight pressing against my back. The shape was human, a man's presence so close I could feel his breath. His hands moved with an intent I did not invite, each touch igniting fear deep in my chest.

A whisper brushed my ear — low, almost taunting. I can't remember every word, but I think it was, "You like this, don't you?" The voice was slick, invasive, as if trying to twist my fear into something else.

My body fought back. I struggled to move, to turn, to push away, but it felt like I was pinned to bed. My breath quickened. My heart pounded so hard it felt like it was shaking the mattress.

I kept fighting, refusing to give in, until suddenly — I woke up. The darkness in my room was real, but the presence was gone. Still, my skin burned with the memory of his touch, and my chest was tight with panic. It felt so real.

Reflection (Emotional + Personal Meaning)

When I woke, I lay still, afraid to even turn on the light. I could still feel him. I could still feel it. It wasn't just a dream — my body didn't know the difference.

This dream touched something raw. It reminded me of times when I felt unsafe, unheard, or disrespected. The invasion wasn't just physically, it was emotional, spiritual. It was about control, about someone forcing a narrative on me that I never agreed to.

The more I thought about it, the more it felt like I had encountered a lust demon — an entity that feeds on fear and desire twisted together. There was something unnatural about the way it moved, the way it whispered, as if it wasn't entirely human.

I couldn't shake the feeling that black magic was at work — that this was not random, but a targeted spiritual attack meant to weaken or drain me. Whether it came from someone's ill intent or from a shadow realm I didn't invite, I knew I had to guard myself more fiercely.

It was my fight, my refusal, and my will to resist that finally broke the hold and woke me up.

Symbolic Breakdown

- The Man on My Back → An external force or influence trying to control, overpower, or silence me. Could represent past trauma, a toxic person, or a spiritual entity.

- The Whisper → Manipulation, gaslighting, or distortion of truth. A voice trying to make me question my own feelings.

- Being Pinned → Feeling powerless in waking life or trapped in a situation I didn't choose.

- Fighting Back → My inner strength and refusal to surrender, even when it feels hopeless.

- Waking Up → Regaining clarity, breaking free from a grip — whether physical, emotional, or spiritual.

Integration Exercise

Think about a time you felt powerless, even if only for a moment. What gave you the strength to resist?

_____
_____
_____
_____

What did you learn about your own boundaries in that moment? Write down one affirmation that affirms your right to safety, autonomy, and power. Example: "My body and my spirit belong to me alone. I am not for the taking."

_____

_____

_____

_____

Think of a Time You Felt Spiritually or Emotionally Pressured

_____

_____

_____

_____

_____

Recall an experience where something or someone tried to influence you against your will. Describe the Tactics Used. Was it manipulation, flattery, intimidation, or twisting of truth? Write them down.

_____

_____

_____

_____

_____

Identify Your Reaction. How did your spirit, body, and mind respond in that moment?

_____

_____

_____

_____

_____

Write a Protection Statement. One or two sentences declaring your right to peace and safety in your mind, body, and spirit.

_____

_____

_____
_____
_____
_____

Affirm Your Spiritual Authority

"I reject every voice and presence that does not come from God. My rest, my mind, and my spirit belong to Him alone."

Spiritual Protection Notes

1. Pray Against Spiritual Intrusion

   o "No unclean spirit has authority over me. My rest is guarded by the most high."

2. Read Your Bible

   o Ephesians 6:10-18 (Armor of God), Psalm 4:8 (peaceful rest).

3. Cleanse Your Sleeping Space

   o Anoint your pillow with a drop of oil while speaking peace and protection.

4. Cleanse Your Body

   o Salt bath before bed to remove negative energy.

5. Play Worship or Scripture Audio While Sleeping

   o Keep your spiritual atmosphere filled with light.

6. Close the Gate

- ○ "No spirit of lust, fear, or manipulation may approach me. My mind and body are sanctified."

The Knock at the Door:

Dream Description

I was in my old house in Delaware, the one that still carries pieces of my childhood. I was in the living room, playing with my cousin. He was about ten years old — just like when we were kids — but I was my current age, twenty-eight.

We laughed and played, the room holding a mix of old memories and my adult awareness. Then came a knock at the door. Firm, steady.

I went to answer it. Standing there was my cousin — but this time he was older, closer to his real age now. My hand reached for the knob, but something didn't feel right. He was already in the house with me, so how could he be at the door?

I asked, "Who is it?" but he didn't answer. He just kept knocking. Then he walked away.

As he moved, his body twisted into something else — a shape that didn't belong to any person I knew. A dark, unrecognizable demon-like figure. My skin prickled.

A moment later, he returned, back in the form of my cousin, pounding on the door harder, faster, with a force that rattled me. This time it wasn't just knocking — it was demanding to be let in.

Fear surged through me. I turned away from the door and told my mom, "I'm going upstairs to get my gun."

And then I woke up.

Reflection

This dream blended the familiar with the frightening. My childhood home and my cousin — both safe places in memory — became shadows of themselves. Seeing him in two places at once told me something was off.

When he transformed into a demon-like figure, my spirit knew he wasn't who he appeared to be. It felt like a test, or a warning, about deception — about forces that can wear the face of someone you trust to gain access to you.

The knocking felt symbolic of something or someone trying to enter my life without permission, breaking boundaries, and disguising their true nature. The fact that I went for my gun showed that even in the dream, I had the instinct to protect myself and stand my ground.

A part of me believes this was more than a dream — it felt like a spiritual attack disguised as something familiar. My spirit discerned it, even before my mind could process it.

Symbolic Breakdown

- Childhood Home → The foundation of who I am; memories and vulnerabilities from my early life.

- Cousin in Two Forms → Trust and familiarity mixed with deception; someone or something taking a trusted form to get close.

- The Knock at the Door → An invitation or temptation; the act of trying to gain entry into your personal or spiritual space.

- The Demon Figure → Hidden danger, spiritual warfare, or unclean energy masked behind a familiar face.

- Getting the Gun → Preparedness, self-defense, and taking power back in a moment of fear.

Integration Exercise

Think of a time someone tried to enter your life — physically, emotionally, or spiritually — without respecting your boundaries. How did you know they weren't who they appeared to be?

_____
_____
_____
_____
_____

What actions did you take to protect yourself?

_____
_____
_____
_____
_____

Write a short declaration of spiritual authority over your own space. Example: "I decide who and what is allowed into my life. Anything that comes with harm or deception will be turned away."

_____
_____
_____
_____
_____

Identify the Disguise. Write about how it presented itself at first — friendly, familiar, helpful — and how that differed from its true nature.

_____
_____
_____
_____
_____

Set Your Spiritual Door Rules. Describe what qualities or intentions someone must have before you let them into your personal or emotional space.

_____
_____
_____
_____
_____

Visualizing Closing the Door. Imagine saying "no" firmly and locking the door on anything that isn't meant for you. Write about how that feels.

_____
_____
_____
_____
_____
_____
_____

Affirm Your Boundaries

"I have authority over my space. Only what is meant for my good and aligned with divine truth may enter my life."

Spiritual Protection Notes

1. Pray or Speak Authority Over Your Home

   o "Every doorway to my home and spirit is sealed in divine light. No deception or harm may enter."

2. Read Your Bible

   o Psalm 91 for protection, 1 John 4:1 for testing spirits.

3. Cleanse the Physical Doorways

   o Wipe doorframes with blessed or anointing oil while praying for safety.

4. Cleanse Your Space

   o Burn sage or incense in a clockwise motion around your home.

5. Visualize Spiritual Boundaries

   o See a wall of light surrounding your home in prayer.

6. Close the Gate

   o "Every false spirit that comes in disguise is turned away. Only truth and love may enter."

When the Smile Shifted:

Dream Description

The dream began lightheartedly. I was in the car with my friend, music flowing through the speakers, windows down, and laughter filling the space. I was driving, she was in the passenger seat, and it felt like one of those perfect moments — no pressure, just joy.

We talked about nothing and everything, singing along to the music, the kind of ride that feels like it could last forever.

Then, without warning, the energy shifted. The air still carried the sound of laughter, but it had a different weight now. She turned toward me and, with a smile, flashed her breasts.

I froze. My mind stumbled over itself — confused because I've never looked at her in that way, never thought of her in a sexual context. The cheerful atmosphere felt strained now, like something was being pushed into the space between us.

Before I could fully process what was happening, she seemed to change. Not just in energy, but in presence — as if she was no longer herself, but someone else entirely. The new presence was insistent, leaning toward me with a clear sexual intent, pushing the moment past what felt natural or safe.

The joy of the ride was gone. I felt caught between disbelief and discomfort, not knowing what would happen next... and then I woke up.

Reflection

When I woke, I was unsettled. I kept replaying the moment — the way the mood changed so quickly and the feeling that the person beside me wasn't truly my friend anymore.

Part of me believes this was symbolic rather than literal. It felt like a message about hidden intentions, or about people in my life who might carry one face but hold another motive underneath. The shift from laughter to discomfort reminded me that not every cheerful connection stays pure, and sometimes spiritual or emotional boundaries are tested when you least expect it.

There was also a strange, almost manipulative energy in the dream — as if a spirit or influence had taken on the familiar image of my friend to get close enough to cross my boundaries. I've had dreams before that felt like spiritual temptations disguised as people I know, and this carried that same uneasy energy.

Symbolic Breakdown

- The Car Ride → A journey shared with someone in your life; the path you're on together.

- Laughter and Music → Joy, connection, and lighthearted moments.

- The Sudden Energy Shift → A change in dynamics, hidden intentions surfacing.

- Flashing Her Breasts → Sexual provocation or testing of boundaries; not necessarily about the person themselves, but about temptation or distraction.

- Transformation into Someone Else → Disguise, deception, or spiritual interference.

- Insistence on Sexual Contact → Pressures or temptations that try to override your personal values and boundaries.

Integration Exercise

Think about a time when the mood of a relationship or situation changed suddenly. Did you feel pressured to go along with something you didn't want?

_____
_____
_____
_____
_____

How did you assert your boundaries? Write down one affirmation of your right to keep relationships within the boundaries you choose. Example: "My comfort matters. My boundaries are not negotiable."

_____
_____
_____
_____
_____
_____
_____

Spiritual Protection Notes

1 Pray or Speak Protection Out Loud
   - "I reject every spirit of temptation and manipulation. No weapon formed against my mind or body shall prosper."

2 Read Your Bible

   - Scriptures for purity and discernment: 1 Corinthians 6:18-20, Proverbs 4:23, Psalm 51:10.

3 Cleanse Your Space

   - Burn sage, palo santo, or incense.

   - Speak blessings over your home and relationships.

4 Cleanse Your Body

   - Salt bath or shower while praying for renewal of mind and spirit.

5 Anoint Yourself

   - Olive or anointing oil on your forehead and heart while asking for protection from deceptive influences.

6 Close the Gate

   - "I seal my relationships and interactions in truth and love. Only those with pure intentions may walk with me."

Holding Through the Pain:

Dream Description

I had just arrived in her city, my heart pounding in anticipation. I was there to meet my Karmic Soul Tie — maybe even my twin flame. She was beautiful, radiant, the kind of beauty that felt familiar, like I had known her forever.

We saw each other from a distance and ran forward with our arms wide open. She jumped into my arms, and I caught her, lifting her high and squeezing her tight. We kissed for what felt like hours, smiling so hard my cheeks ached. Her hands cupped my face as we stared into each other's eyes — it was as if time didn't exist.

The atmosphere was intoxicating. A breath of fresh air. Like we were floating on cloud nine, surrounded by invisible hearts and butterflies spinning around our heads. She wrapped her legs around my waist, and I held her closer, refusing to let go.

Then, without warning, there was a shift. I heard a sound — a faint scratch against the pillow by my head. I was asleep and so lost in the dream that I ignored it, choosing to stay in that bliss.

But then I felt a dull pain in my back. At first, I brushed it off. I didn't want to lose the moment. But the sensation deepened. It felt like sharp nails pressing hard into my back, digging deeper.

The pain grew sharper, more violent. In the dream, I started screaming, the sound torn between pleasure and agony. Yet neither of us let go. I clung to her, and she to me. But now I could see concern in her face — the joy had dimmed, replaced by fear for me.

The pain became unbearable, a piercing force that ripped me out of my sleep. I woke up gasping, my hands rushing to my back. My room was dark. Silent. No one was there.

Reflection

This dream was both bliss and torment — pure love entwined with sudden pain. My Karmic Soul Tie felt like home, like safety, but the pain reminded me that even deep connections can carry wounds.

Part of me wonders if this was more than a dream — maybe a visitation, or even a spiritual entanglement where both love and unresolved karmic energy coexist. The way I ignored the pain at first reminds me of moments in waking life where I've overlooked harm to hold onto love.

The scratch by my head and the nails in my back made me think of spiritual interference — an outside force trying to corrupt a pure moment. In karmic and twin flame journeys, outside energies sometimes test the bond, especially when two souls are deeply aligned.

Symbolic Breakdown

- Her City Arrival → Entering a new chapter or reconnecting with a significant soul connection.

- Running & Embracing → Desire for reunion, emotional safety, deep love.

- Cloud Nine Atmosphere → Spiritual high, unconditional joy.

- Scratching Sound → Spiritual disturbance, warning, or interference.

- Back Pain & Nails Digging → Hidden wounds, spiritual attack, or karmic lessons surfacing.

- Refusing to Let Go → Attachment, loyalty, or the inability to release a bond even when it causes harm.

Integration Exercise

Think of a relationship — romantic, platonic, or familial — that brought both joy and pain. Did you ever ignore warning signs to preserve the good moments?

_____
_____
_____
_____
_____
_____

How did that affect you in the long run?

_____
_____
_____
_____

Write one affirmation about balancing love with self-protection.
Example: "I can love deeply without allowing harm to remain in
my space."

_____
_____
_____
_____
_____
_____

Spiritual Protection Notes

1. Pray or Speak Protection Out Loud

   o "I break any cords or connections that bring pain
     into my life. I keep only what is aligned with love,
     light, and divine truth."

2. Read Your Bible

   o Scriptures for love and spiritual safeguarding: 1
     Corinthians 13, Psalm 91, Ephesians 6:10-18.

3. Cleanse Your Space

   o Burn sage, palo santo, or incense.

   o Walk through your home declaring protection over
     every room.

4. Cleanse Your Body

- o Take a salt bath or shower while visualizing the pain and heaviness washing away.

5. Anoint Yourself

   - o Apply oil to your forehead, heart, and back while praying for release from spiritual interference.

6. Close the Gate

   - o "I seal every doorway in my dreams and in my spirit that does not come from God. Only truth, love, and divine guidance may remain."

The Cliff and the Ocean

I can't remember how it began — just that I was with my mother in Delaware, laughing, talking, existing in the safety of her presence. My phone buzzed in my hand, pulling me out of the moment. The alert made my heart jolt: my Karmic Soul-Tie — my possible twin flame — her location had been tagged.

She was in California, driving along a winding mountain road.

Physically, I was still there in Delaware with my mom… but in spirit, I was hovering over her car, as if the thread between us had pulled me to her. I could see everything — the curve of the mountain ahead, the jagged cliff waiting at the end, and far below, the vast expanse of ocean.

My chest tightened. She was heading straight toward the edge.

I shouted for her in my mind, reached for my phone, tried to call — but before my voice could reach her, she drove off.

I braced myself for the plunge, for the crash, for the violent pull of the ocean swallowing her whole. But instead… the car floated. Resting lightly on top of the water like the impossible was just another Tuesday.

I called her, my voice trembling with fear and urgency.

"Are you okay?!"

Her reply was unnervingly calm — nonchalant, almost careless. No fear. No awareness of how close she was to death.

I told her to hold on, that I'd call for help. I hung up and dialed 911, words spilling out in a rush — but the dispatcher's tone was detached. "I have other important calls. I can't help you," she said, and hung up.

My hands shook with rage and disbelief.

Someone I loved was in extreme danger, and no one cared.

I called back my twin flame again — still the same flat, distant energy. But this time the water was creeping higher, slipping into the car. Time was running out.

I called 911 again, this time with fire in my voice. I demanded help, my words sharp and unyielding. The dispatcher finally caught the weight of my tone and asked for her location. I gave it to her without hesitation. She said help was on the way.

I called my Twin Flame again, desperate to know if she was still alive. Relief flooded me when she answered — but the clock was still ticking. This time, her voice carried a flicker of urgency, a shift in energy. She started to move, to try to escape before the car was swallowed completely.

And just as the water began to rise over her head — I woke up.

Reflection

This dream left me with a knot in my stomach — a mix of helplessness, urgency, and frustration. It was the kind of dream that doesn't fade when you open your eyes. I could still feel the weight of my phone in my hand, the dispatcher's indifference, and the image of her car bobbing on the water while the ocean waited to pull it under.

It reminded me that sometimes, even when you see danger ahead, you can't make someone care enough to save themselves. You can try to warn them, you can fight for them, but if they aren't ready to fight too, your hands will always feel tied.

Symbolic Breakdown

- The Mountain Road – Represents the life path of your Karmic Soul-Tie, filled with twists, elevation, and unseen dangers.

- The Cliff – A breaking point; a moment of no return where choices lead to irreversible outcomes.

- The Ocean – Symbolizes the unconscious, deep emotions, and spiritual transformation — but also overwhelming forces that can consume.

- The Floating Car – A temporary illusion of safety; surviving a fall but not truly out of danger.

- Nonchalant Attitude – Emotional detachment, denial, or spiritual unawareness of the danger at hand.

- 911 Dispatcher Hanging Up – External help being unavailable or unwilling; the reminder that not everyone will see your emergency as urgent.

- Calling Back with Authority – Stepping into your power and using your voice to demand action — symbolic of spiritual authority and standing in your truth.

Integration Exercise

Journal Prompt: Write about a time you saw someone heading toward self-destruction and couldn't stop them. How did you respond? How did it affect you emotionally and spiritually?

_____
_____
_____
_____
_____
_____

Energy Visualization: Imagine standing on a safe shore, holding a bright lifeline of light. See yourself casting it toward someone in the water — without jumping in yourself. Feel the balance of compassion without drowning in their chaos.

_____
_____
_____
_____
_____
_____

Affirmation: "I can love deeply without losing myself. I can call for help without taking on the weight of saving everyone."

_____
_____

_____
_____
_____
_____

Action Step: Identify one situation in your current life where you may be overextending yourself emotionally. Practice setting one clear boundary this week.

_____
_____
_____
_____
_____
_____
_____

Spiritual Protection Notes

- Cord Cutting Ritual: Perform a gentle cord-cutting meditation to clear any unhealthy energetic ties without erasing the lessons or love.

- Before sleeping, ask for divine guidance and protection in your dreams.

- When you dream of someone in danger, pray for their safety and release them into God's hands.

- Use Psalm 91 as a nightly covering over yourself and your loved ones.

- Saltwater Cleanse: Use a salt bath or saltwater foot soak to release lingering emotional heaviness from the dream.

- Protective Visualization: Before sleep, imagine yourself surrounded by a sphere of golden light that nothing harmful can penetrate.

- Prayer/Mantra: "Spirit, protect my energy and guide my heart to act from love, not fear. Show me when to hold on and when to let go."

Dreams became another classroom for my healing and faith. After I learned about spiritual warfare and inner healing, God started visiting me in the night. What I couldn't see clearly that day, He revealed in my sleep.

Some dreams exposed the people around me — showing me who was for me and who was against me. Others mirrored my inner struggles, with broken houses, storms, or empty rooms symbolizing the places inside me that still needed God's restoration. And then there were the dreams that gave me hope: visions of light, of breakthroughs, of promises waiting on the other side of my pain.

At first, I didn't know what to do with them. But scripture reminded me that I wasn't alone — God had always spoken to His people through dreams.

- Joseph was shown his destiny through dreams (Genesis 37:5–10).

- Daniel was given wisdom to interpret visions and mysteries (Daniel 2:19).

- Even in Job, it says: "For God speaks again and again... He speaks in dreams, in visions of the night, when deep sleep falls on people as they lie in their beds" (Job 33:14–15).

My dreams weren't random. They were warnings, confirmations, and sometimes healing encounters with God's presence. What the enemy tried to confuse me with through black magic and fear; God was countering with truth and revelation while I rested.

As I look back on these dreams, I see more than strange images and impossible events. I see guidance, warnings, and mirrors reflecting pieces of my own journey. Each vision, no matter how unsettling or beautiful, has shaped the way I move through life in the waking world.

The dream realm has taught me that not all battles are fought with words or actions — some are fought in silence, in symbols, in space between worlds. And when I return from those places, I bring back more than memories. I bring back wisdom, strength, and the understanding that nothing in my spiritual walk is random.

I step out of each dream knowing that what I have seen was meant for me — to heal me, to warn me, or to prepare me. And now, I share these visions with you, so that the messages that found me in the night might also find a place in your heart.

Reflection & Prayer

Scriptures to Meditate On

- *"For God speaks again and again... He speaks in dreams, in visions of the night." – Job 33:14–15*

- *"Your old men will dream dreams, your young men will see visions." – Joel 2:28*

- *"Surely the Sovereign Lord does nothing without revealing his plan to his servants the prophets." – Amos 3:7*

Questions for Reflection

1. What is one dream you've had that felt more like a message than a random thought?

_____

_____

_____

_____

_____

_____

2. Did it warn you, comfort you, or reveal something hidden?

_____

_____

_____

_____

_____

3. How might God be using your dreams as a guide for your healing or direction today?

_____

_____

_____

_____

_____

_____

4. Have you ever had a dream that stayed with you, even after you woke up? What do you think God might have been showing you through it?

_____

_____

_____

_____

_____

5. Do you pay attention to patterns in your dreams — like recurring themes, people, or places?

_____

_____

_____

_____

_____

_____

6. How can you invite God into your dream life, asking Him for clarity and peace instead of fear or confusion?

_____

_____

_____

_____

_____

_____

Closing Prayer

Heavenly Father,

thank You for speaking to me even in the night. Thank You that while I rest, you are still working and revealing the truth. Help me to discern Your voice through my dreams, and to receive them not with fear, but with faith. Guard my heart from confusion and deception and fill me with peace and wisdom as I continue this journey.

In Jesus' name, Amen.

Dreams were never just dreams for me — they were God's whispers in the night, preparing me for a greater awakening. Each vision, each symbol, each message brought me one step closer to what He really wanted me to see: my divine clarity and purpose.

CHAPTER SIX
Last's Night Dream Journal

Setting Place: Where were you?

_____

_____

Main People Characters: Who showed up?

_____

_____

Symbols Objects: What stood out?

_____

_____

Emotions Felt: During & after.

_____

_____

Write one sentence that sums up the
dream's 'atmosphere.

_____

_____

"God speaks once, yes twice, yet man perceives it not...
In a dream, in a vision of the night." – Job 33:14-15

Symbol Decoder wheel

In the circle's center, write one powerful dream symbol (house, storm, snake, door, baby, etc).

What does this symbol mean to me personally?

What does this symbol mean in Bibe / spiritually?

Symbol

What does this symbol were tied to it in the dream?

What might God be saying through it?

What might God be saying through it?

"The Spirit searches all things, even the deep things of God."-1 Cor. 2:10

The Dream House Reflection

Imagine your dream house as a picture of your heart/soul.
Label the rooms and fill in:

Room 1
What part of me feels
broken or abandoned?

Room 2
What part of me
feels restored or
safe?

Room 3
What might God
be saying God's
healing?

Unless the Lord builds the house, those who
build it labor in vain.'- Psalm 127:1

Spiritual Discernment Test

For your dream, list what evidence shows it is from:

God / Higher Self:

- Peace
- Clarity
- Warning
- Confirmation

The Enemy / Confusion:

- Fear
- Chaos
- Contraction
- Condemnation

What fruit does this dream
produce in me – fear or faith?

_____

_____

_____

_____

"You will know them by their fruits." – Matthew
7:16

Doorway Dream Exercise

Imagine each dream as a doorway. Write:

What door opened in my dream?
(relationship, new opportunity,
hidden truth)

What door closed?
(toxic tie, old wound, false belief)

_____

_____

_____

What step am I being asked
to take in waking life?

_____

_____

_____

_____

"See, I have set before you an open door, which no
one can shut." – Rev. 3:8

Dream to Action Plan

Write the most recent dream that felt like a
warning or message.

What is God preparing me for?

_____

_____

_____

What steps can I take now?

_____

_____

_____

Who should I pray for
based on this dream?

_____

_____

_____

Lord, thank You for speaking in visions.
Help me walk in wisdom with what You've
shown me.

Lord, thank You for speaking in visions.
- Matthew 7:16

Chapter 7: Divine Clarity and Purpose

Coming out of the season of dreams, I began to see why God allowed me to even watch the psychic readings in the first place. God knew that. He knew my heart, my search, and the places where I was willing to listen. So, he met me where I was. He used what mattered most to me — the person I believed was my twin flame — to open my eyes and draw me closer to Him.

Through that experience, I came face-to-face with the reality of spiritual warfare. Every single day, as divine beings, we are under attack. The enemy doesn't come at us with obvious weapons. He comes for the heart — for whatever means the most to us. For me, it was love. The devil wanted me bitter. He wanted me depressed, shut off, cold-hearted, unwilling to trust again.

But here's the truth: even after all the pain my karmic ex caused me, I did not allow myself to become cold-hearted toward the one I thought was my twin flame. Instead, God used that test to see if I would keep my heart open. And I did. But He also had to teach me something deeper — how to put myself first, how to place boundaries on my love, and how to let Him shape me into my divine purpose.

That's why I'm writing this book. To teach and guide others. To remind you that love — real love, God's love — is the only way back to Him.

Even while I continued to watch the readings and prayed, asking God, "What are You showing me?" He revealed another lesson: I was being prepared to help others heal. To help them understand that love is the doorway to him.

Along the way, I learned that both men and women carry feminine and masculine energy. Feminine energy relates to our emotions, while masculine energy relates to our logical thinking. When we lead only with logic, we lean on the mind — and the enemy loves to twist and confuse our thoughts. But when we lead with the heart, we open ourselves to God, because both the mind and heart belong to Him. (Jeremiah 17:10 – "I the Lord search the heart and examine the mind, to reward each person according to their conduct, according to what their deeds deserve.")

As a child, I used to think Jesus was like a superhero, snapping His fingers to heal people. But as I grew, I came to understand that Jesus was God incarnate — God in human form — showing us the way. (John 1:14 – "The Word became flesh and made his dwelling among us.") He walked as one of us, pouring love into strangers, healing, and praying.

And now, we are called to continue His work. We are His disciples. Our testimonies matter. Our spiritual journeys matter. We are meant to share them so others can awaken to who God really is and to the mission of being saved.

God is within us. He is the balance of yin and yang, night and day, light and dark, love and hate, heart and mind. Once we understand this, we begin to hear Him more clearly through discernment and intuition.

In that understanding, I also came to see that relationships are not accidents. There are givers and takers in our lives, and both play a divine role. Some people are placed in our path to pour into us, to remind us of love, patience, or sacrifice. Others come to challenge us, drain us, or expose wounds we still need to heal. But even those who hurt us carry purpose, because God uses every encounter for our growth.

Not everyone is meant to stay forever. Some people are here only for a reason — to teach us a lesson, to shift our path, or to awaken something in us. Others are here for a season — they walk with us for a time, shaping our story before their chapter closes. And then there are those rare souls who are here for a lifetime — the ones who remain through trials, growth, and change, woven into the fabric of our journey.

When I started to see relationships through this lens, I realized nothing was wasted. Every giver and taker, every reason, season, and lifetime bond was divinely placed to mold me into who I am becoming. And above all, I remembered the truth that anchors it all: God is love.

To truly hear Him, we must heal, learn how to give and receive love, and walk in it every day. (1 John 4:16 – "God is love. Whoever lives in love lives in God, and God in them.") To hear Him clearly, we must heal. We must learn how to give and receive love. And we must choose, every day, to walk in it. That's where divine clarity and purpose are born.

Your Turn to Reflect

Scriptures to Meditate On

- *Jeremiah 17:10 – "I the Lord search the heart and examine the mind, to reward each person according to their conduct, according to what their deeds deserve."*

- *John 1:14 – "The Word became flesh and made his dwelling among us."*

- *1 John 4:16 – "God is love. Whoever lives in love lives in God, and God in them."*

- *Romans 12:2 – "Do not conform to the pattern of this world, but be transformed by the renewing of your mind."*

Reflection Questions

Looking back, has there been a time where God used something painful to draw you closer to Him?

_____

_____

_____

_____

In what ways have you allowed the enemy to use your mind (logic, doubt, fear) to silence your heart?

_____

_____

_____

_____

_____

How can you set healthy boundaries in love that honor both God and yourself?

_____

_____

_____

_____

_____

What does it mean to you personally that "God is love"? How could you live this truth out daily?

_____

_____

_____

_____

_____

Who in your life might need to hear your testimony, so that they too can be reminded of God's love?

_____

_____

_____

_____

_____

_____

_____

_____

Closing Prayer

Heavenly Father, Thank You for turning even my heartbreak into lessons that lead me closer to You. Help me to guard my heart, renew my mind, and walk in the truth that You are love. Teach me to balance wisdom with compassion, logic with faith, and to set boundaries that honor who You created me to be. Fill me with discernment, so that I may hear Your voice above all others. Use my testimony not just for my healing, but to help others see Your light through me. I surrender my heart, my mind, and my journey back to You.

In Jesus' name, Amen.

Mapping My Relationships

1. On the Reason branch: Write names of people who came into your life just to teach you something. Next to each, write the lesson. Example: Taught me patience, showed me my worth, helped me discover my strength.

2. On the Season branch: Write those who walked with you for a while, but eventually left. Note how that chapter shaped you. 3. On the Lifetime branch: Write the names of those still present — your anchors, soul connections, or family. Write why they remain important. Footer Quote: "There is a time for everything, and a season for every activity under the heavens." – Ecclesiastes 3:1

Reason

_____

_____

Learn...

Learn...
_____

_____

Lifetime

I care...
_____

_____

Taught me...
_____

_____

Write why...
_____

_____

There is a timefor everything, and a season for every activity under the heavens."- Ecclesiastes 3:1

Givers & Takers Reflection

Write people(pastor present) who poured into you.Next to each, describe what they gave(love,wisdom,laughter, protection). Write people who drained you. Nexto each, describe what they revealed about your boundaries, self-worth, or lessons.

Givers	Takers

What patterns do I notice? How can I honor the givers and set boundaries with the takers?

Even takers can teach. Even givers can be a mirror of God's love.

Boundaries as Love

Write 5 boundaries that help you protect My Peace.

Example petals: Time, Energy, Words, Heart, Body.
In each, write one specific boundary. Example: Time→
I will not overextend myself to please others.

My Peace

_____   _____
_____   _____
_____

"Above all else, guard your heart, for everything you
do flows from it."-Proverbs 4:23

Divine Balance: Heart vs. Mind

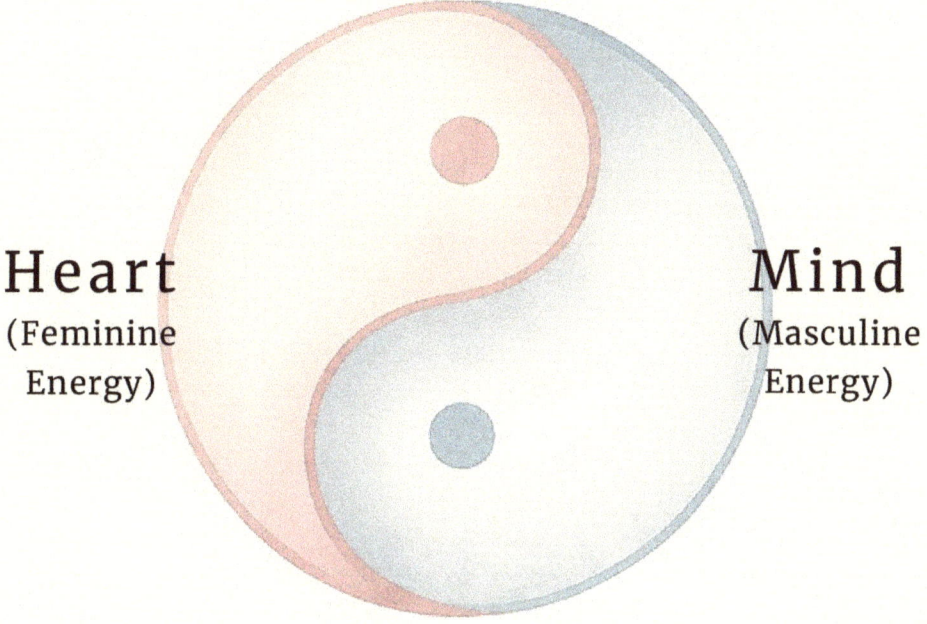

Heart
(Feminine
Energy)

Mind
(Masculine
Energy)

Write how you can lead
with compassion, love,
and vulnerability.

Write how you can lead with
wisdom, discernment,
and logic.

_____

_____

_____

Where do I lean too much—and how can I balance?

_____

"I the Lord search the heart and examine the mind."
-Jeremiah 17:10

My Purpose Statement

God is calling me to...

_____

_____

The pain I've endured has
prepared me to...

_____

_____

The love I carry will...

_____

_____

My purpose is...

_____

_____

Signed with faith, _____

"For I know the plans I have for you... plans to
give you hope and a future." – Jeremiah 29:11

The Message Before the Journey

A Blessing for the Journey

If you made it to this page, I want you to know something important: you are already healing. The fact that you chose to pick up these words, to sit with your own pain instead of running from it, is proof that God is at work in you.

Your story doesn't end with rejection, heartbreak, or confusion. Those were only chapters — not your whole book. The Author of your life is still writing, and His pen has never run dry. May you walk away from these pages not just with lessons, but with clarity.

Clarity about who you are.

Clarity about what love is.

Clarity about the God who has been with you every step of the way.

I bless you with peace, with hope, with courage to open your heart again.

I bless you with discernment to recognize love that reflects God's heart.

And I bless you with the faith to know that your best chapters are still ahead.

Take this with you: You are loved. You are chosen. You are never alone.

Beloved, you've just walked with me through stories of pain, lessons, and healing. But now this part is no longer about me — it's about you.

These next pages are designed to help you:

- Reflect on your own journey.

- Process your pain in the light of God's truth.

- Discover what He wants to reveal about your heart, your healing, and your future.

Think of this section as a conversation between you and God. Be honest, be unfiltered, and let the Spirit guide you. There are no wrong answers here. Every word you write is a step toward deeper healing.

As you begin, keep this scripture close:

"Draw near to God and He will draw near to you." – James 4:8

Take a deep breath. Quiet your spirit.

Invite God into this moment.

And then — begin writing.

A Prayer of Invitation

Heavenly Father,

As I begin this journey of reflection, I invite
You into these pages and into my heart.
Help me to see myself the way You see me —
loved, worthy, and whole.
Give me courage to be honest with my words
and bold in facing my truth.
Where there is pain, bring healing.
Where there is confusion, bring clarity.
Where there is brokenness, bring restoration.

Let every question I answer and every thought I write
down draw me closer to You.
Remind me that I am never alone in this process —
for You are with me, guiding me, and healing me.

In Jesus' name, Amen.

Begin with openness.   Begin with God.

Workbook Section: Inner Child & Shadow Self Healing

Up until now, you've walked with me through my story — the heartbreaks, the prayers, the revelations, and the healing. Now, it's your turn. This section is not about me, but about you. Here, you'll meet your own inner child, uncover the parts of yourself you've hidden in the shadows, and allow God to shine light where healing is needed. Take your time. Pray before each section. Write freely. Healing is not a race — it's a journey. (More journal space in the back of book)

Part One: Meeting Your Inner Child

Reflection Questions
1. What is your earliest memory of feeling loved?

_____

_____

_____

_____

_____

2. What is your earliest memory of feeling abandoned or unseen?

_____

_____

_____

_____

_____

3. As a child, what did you need most from your parents, caregivers, or community? Did you receive it?

_____

_____

_____

_____

_____

4. What words or beliefs did you carry from childhood that still echo in your life today?

_____
_____
_____
_____
_____
_____
_____
_____

5. If you could speak to your younger self right now, what would you say?

_____
_____
_____
_____
_____

Silence as Survival
Think back to a time in your childhood when you stayed quiet instead of speaking up.

What did your silence protect you from? What feelings were you holding back?

_____
_____
_____
_____
_____
_____
_____
_____
_____

Reclaiming Your Voice
If you could go back to that younger version of you, what words of love, truth, or protection would you speak over them?

_____
_____
_____
_____
_____

Write as if you are speaking directly to the younger you who stayed silent when people made fun of you.

I remember when you felt _____ (hurt, alone, angry)."

"You chose not to speak up because _____ (what were you afraid of, what were you protecting?)."

"I want you to know now that _____ (give comfort, reassurance, or love)."

If you could have had someone defend you in that moment, what would you have wanted them to say?"

Exercise

✎. Write a letter to your younger self. Tell them what you wish they knew back then. Offer comfort, guidance, and remind them of their worth.

_____
_____
_____
_____
_____
_____
_____
_____
_____
_____
_____
_____
_____

_____
_____
_____
_____
_____
_____
_____
_____
_____
_____
_____
_____
_____
_____
_____
_____
_____
_____
_____
_____
_____
_____

Scripture Meditation

Psalm 34:18 – "The Lord is close to the brokenhearted and saves those who are crushed in spirit."

Matthew 18:3 – "Truly I tell you, unless you change and become like little children, you will never enter the kingdom of heaven."

Part Two: Exploring Your Shadow Self

Reflection Questions

1. What parts of yourself do you tend to hide from others? Why?

_____

_____

_____

_____

_____

2. What emotions are the hardest for you to express (anger, sadness, fear, vulnerability)?

_____

_____

_____

_____

3. In what ways have you been self-protective that may now be limiting your growth?

_____

_____

_____

_____

_____

4. What patterns do you notice repeating in your relationships?

_____

_____

_____

_____

_____

5. What triggers you most — and what do those triggers reveal about wounds you've carried?

_____

_____

_____

_____

_____

How do you notice those silences showing up in your adult life today?

Do you find yourself speaking words now that your younger self could not?

_____

_____

_____

_____

_____

How can you honor that child by using your voice differently today?

_____

_____

_____

_____

_____

Now, let the part of you that held the anger and silence speak. These are written as your shadow speaking to you, in "I" statements.

"I am the part of you that feels ____."

"I stayed hidden because ____."

"What I really wanted to do back then was ____."

"If you let me out in healthy ways today, I could give you ____ (power, strength, fire, courage)."

Exercise

✎ Draw or describe your shadow self. Think of it not as evil, but as parts of you waiting to be healed and accepted by God.

_____
_____
_____
_____
_____
_____
_____
_____
_____
_____
_____
_____
_____
_____
_____
_____
_____
_____
_____
_____
_____
_____
_____
_____
_____
_____
_____
_____
_____
_____
_____
_____
_____
_____
_____

Scripture Meditation

John 1:5 – "The light shines in the darkness, and the darkness has not overcome it."

2 Corinthians 12:9 – "My grace is sufficient for you, for my power is made perfect in weakness."

Part Three: Integration & Healing

Reflection Questions

1. How can you begin to nurture your inner child today?

_____

_____

_____

_____

_____

2. What boundaries can you set that honor both your shadow and your light?

_____

_____

_____

_____

_____

3. What does "wholeness" look like for you in this season of your life?

_____

_____

_____

_____

_____

_____

_____

_____

4. How has God already been showing you glimpses of healing?

_____

_____

_____

_____

_____

_____

5. What step will you take this week to walk toward that healing?

_____

_____

_____

_____

Finish by writing as your present self:

"Thank you, inner child, for showing me ____."

"Thank you, shadow, for protecting me by ____."

"Here's how I will honor both of you moving forward: ____ (example: speaking up for myself, journaling my anger, using my voice when I feel disrespected)."

Exercise
✎ Create an affirmation for your healing journey. Write it down and repeat it daily. Example: "I am loved, I am chosen, and I am whole in God's eyes."

_____

_____

_____

_____

_____

_____

_____

_____

_____

_____

_____

_____

_____

_____

_____

_____

_____

Scripture Meditation

Isaiah 61:3 – "...to bestow on them a crown of beauty instead of ashes, the oil of joy instead of mourning, and a garment of praise instead of a spirit of despair."

Philippians 1:6 – "Being confident of this, that He who began a good work in you will carry it on to completion until the day of Christ Jesus."

Voices Without Boundaries
Share your truth

Use these next few lines to share your story—whether it's a whisper from your heart or a roar of strength. Every word you write matters. By pouring your truth onto these pages, you create something lasting, something that will inspire and guide the next reader who turns them.

Definitions

Key Spiritual Terms

Twin Flame

A soul connection believed to be the "other half" of one's spirit. The bond is often intense, magnetic, and transformative — meant to awaken deep growth, whether or not the relationship lasts.

Karmic Partner

A relationship designed to teach hard lessons and reveal patterns that must be broken. Often painful, these connections help you confront cycles of hurt and prepare for healthier love.

Soulmate

A soul connection rooted in harmony and unconditional support. Soulmates can be romantic, platonic, or even family bonds. Unlike twin flames, soulmates bring peace, balance, and companionship without constant turmoil.

Kindred Spirit

Someone whose energy resonates deeply with yours, creating an instant feeling of understanding and comfort. A kindred spirit may not be permanent, but the connection feels natural and affirming.

Divine Counterpart

A spiritually aligned partner chosen by God, often representing His plan for your purpose. Unlike karmic or twin flame intensity, divine counterparts create stability, mutual growth, and faith-based love.

Soul Contract

A spiritual agreement made before birth, where souls choose to meet in this lifetime to fulfill lessons, growth, or healing for one another. Not all contracts are meant to last forever.

Spiritual Awakening Partner

A person who enters your life to trigger awakening — whether through love, pain, or loss. Their role is to shift your perspective and draw you closer to God, even if their presence is temporary.

False Twin Flame

A connection that feels identical to a twin flame but is rooted in illusion. False twins often mirror your wounds without leading to growth, keeping you stuck in confusion until clarity comes.

Catalyst

A person whose presence ignites rapid spiritual growth and transformation, often through heartbreak, rejection, or sudden separation. A catalyst awakens dormant parts of your soul, forcing you to confront pain, heal old wounds, and step into your higher purpose. While the connection may feel intense, their role is not to stay, but to spark the change that aligns you with God's plan.

Spiritual & Energetic Concepts

Shadow Work

The practice of facing the hidden, wounded, or denied parts of yourself so you can heal and integrate them.

Soul Tie

A deep energetic bond formed through intimacy, shared trauma, or spiritual connection that lingers long after a relationship ends.

Energy Exchange

The invisible giving and receiving of emotional, spiritual, or physical energy between people. Some connections leave you drained, while others leave you full.

Kundalini Awakening

A surge of spiritual energy that rises through the body, often triggered by a powerful connection or deep prayer/meditation.

Ascension

The process of growing in spiritual awareness, shedding old patterns, and stepping closer to your divine purpose.

Healing

The process of reclaiming your power, restoring your peace, and finding wholeness in God after heartbreak or trauma. Healing turns pain into purpose.

Psychological & Toxic Relational Dynamics

Trauma Bond

An emotional tie formed through cycles of abuse, manipulation, or inconsistency — where love and harm become intertwined.

Gaslighting

A manipulation tactic where someone makes you doubt your own memory, perception, or reality.

Love Bombing

Over-the-top affection and attention at the start of a relationship, designed to hook you emotionally.

Hoovering

When someone who left suddenly tries to pull you back into their cycle of manipulation (like a vacuum sucking you back in).

Projection

When a person accuses you of their very behavior or flaw, they are guilty of themselves.

Ghosting

When someone abruptly ends all communication without explanation. Though deeply painful, ghosting often signals their lack of readiness rather than your lack of worth.

False Hope

Clinging to the possibility of something that contradicts reality. False hope often keeps us chained to the past, while God's truth brings clarity and freedom.

Energy Vampire

A person who drains your emotional, mental, or spiritual energy. They thrive on your attention, compassion, or reactions, often leaving you feeling exhausted, anxious, or depleted after interacting with them. Energy vampires may not always realize what they're doing, but their presence takes more than it gives. Protecting yourself through boundaries and discernment is essential when dealing with them.

Healing & Growth Terms

Inner Child

The younger, vulnerable part of yourself still carries unmet needs, joy, or wounds from childhood.

Reparenting

The act of giving yourself (as an adult) the love, care, and guidance you didn't receive growing up.

Boundaries

The sacred lines you draw to protect your heart, energy, and peace. The healthy limits we set to protect our heart, time, energy, and peace. Boundaries are a form of self-love and spiritual wisdom, reminding us that love must be mutual.

Discernment

The spiritual wisdom to distinguish truth from illusion, God's plan from your own desires.

Alignment

Living in harmony with God's purpose for your life, where your choices, values, and spirit match His path.

Divine Redirection

What feels like rejection or loss is often God's way of removing what isn't aligned with His plan, to prepare the way for something greater.

God's Plan

The promise of Jeremiah 29:11 — that God has plans to prosper you, give you hope, and secure your future. Trusting His plan means surrendering what doesn't serve your destiny.

Sacred Mirror

A person who reflects your deepest truths and wounds back to you, forcing you to face what you'd rather hide.

Soul Lesson

The core teaching a connection or season in life was meant to be revealed.

Divine Timing

The belief that events unfold not when you want, but when God knows you're ready.

Spiritual Warfare

The unseen battles between light and darkness that manifest in relationships, temptations, or inner struggles.

The Surrender

That holy moment when you stop fighting, stop clinging, and release everything to God's will.

Types of Rituals in Religion & Spirituality

Prayer Ritual

The most common religious ritual. Direct communication with God (or the Divine) through words, silence, or meditation. Prayers may involve asking, thanking, praising, or seeking guidance.

Fasting Ritual

Abstaining from food, drink, or certain activities for a set period to purify the body, strengthen discipline, and draw closer to God. Examples include Lent, Ramadan, or personal fasts.

Worship Ritual

Acts of devotion such as singing, dancing, clapping, kneeling, or lifting hands during church or spiritual gatherings. These express reverence and love for God.

Sacrificial Ritual

Offering something valuable (time, resources, or symbolic items) as a way of honoring God or surrendering earthly attachments. In modern faith practice, this is often non-bloody (like tithing or offerings).

Baptism Ritual

A ceremonial washing with water symbolizing purification, rebirth, and dedication to God. Found in Christianity and mirrored in cleansing rites in other faiths.

Communion (Eucharist) Ritual

Sacred sharing of bread and wine (or symbolic substitutes) representing unity with Christ's body and blood. A reminder of sacrifice and covenant.

Pilgrimage Ritual

Travel to a sacred site for worship, reflection, or renewal. Examples: Mecca (Islam), Jerusalem (Christianity/Judaism), Ganges River (Hinduism).

Anointing Ritual

Using oil (or other sacred substance) as a symbol of blessing, healing, or setting someone apart for God's purpose. Common in Christianity and Judaism.

Confession / Repentance Ritual

Admitting sins, asking forgiveness, and turning back toward God. May be done privately in prayer or through a priest/spiritual leader.

Meditation Ritual

Focused silence or reflection to connect with God, inner self, or spiritual truths. Practiced in many traditions (Christian contemplation, Buddhist mindfulness, Hindu dhyana).

Burial / Funeral Rituals

Sacred practices to honor the dead, comfort the living, and commit souls to God's care. Practices vary by religion but are center on remembrance and transition.

Feast / Festival Rituals

Celebrations tied to holy days, honoring God through food, music, dance, and community. Examples: Passover, Easter, Diwali, Eid.

<u>Types of Narcissists</u>

Overt Narcissist

The classic, obvious type. Loud, arrogant, and attention-seeking. They thrive on praise, belittle others openly, and lack empathy in ways that are hard to miss.

Covert Narcissist

Quieter, more hidden. They may appear shy or sensitive but use passive-aggressive tactics, guilt-trips, and victimhood to control others. Their manipulation is subtle but deeply damaging.

Malignant Narcissist

The most destructive form. Combines narcissistic traits with cruelty, aggression, and sometimes sadistic behaviors. They enjoy controlling and hurting others, showing little to no conscience.

Communal Narcissist

Masks selfishness with "good deeds." They seek admiration for being charitable, kind, or spiritual, but their generosity is motivated by recognition, not genuine care.

Somatic Narcissist

Obsessed with body, appearance, sex, or physical attraction. They use their looks or sexuality as tools for validation and manipulation.

Cerebral Narcissist

Seeks superiority through intellect and knowledge. They belittle others by acting as the "smartest in the room" and thrive on making people feel small or ignorant.

Victim Narcissist

Portrays themselves as always wronged, misunderstood, or mistreated. They draw sympathy to manipulate others, refusing accountability while demanding endless emotional labor.

Spiritual Narcissist

Uses religion, spirituality, or "higher knowledge" as a weapon to elevate themselves above others. They may shame people for not being "as enlightened" and hide control under the guise of faith or wisdom.

Epilogue

A Final Blessing to the Reader

Beloved, if you have journeyed with me to these final pages, know this: your story is not over. Every wound, every heartbreak, every unanswered question has not been wasted — it is being transformed into wisdom, strength, and testimony. You are not defined by who left, but by the God who has never left you.

May you walk forward knowing you are chosen, cherished, and destined for greater things than your past could ever hold.

Final Word: Closing Prayer

Heavenly Father,

I thank You for every heart that has held these pages, for every soul who has walked through pain yet chose healing. Let these words not simply rest on paper, but take root as seeds of strength, wisdom, and intimacy with You.

Lord, for every reader, I ask that where there has been heartbreak, you would plant hope. Where there has been confusion, bring clarity. Where there has been rejection, remind them of Your eternal acceptance.

Surround them with people who reflect Your love. Guard their hearts with Your peace. Renew their minds with Your truth. Give them courage to open their hearts again — not to what breaks them, but to what aligns with Your will.

May this not be an ending, but a new beginning — a chapter of purpose, faith, and divine alignment. And may we always remember that You are Love, and Your love never fails.

In Jesus' name,

Amen.

📖 "The Lord will fight for you; you need only to be still." – Exodus 14:14

A Final Letter to You

Dear Beloved,

If you are reading these last words, I want to pause and tell you how proud I am of you. You made it through these pages, but more importantly — you've made it through things in life that once felt unbearable. That is strength. That is courage. That is grace at work within you.

Please remember this: your story is not over. Every scar holds a testimony; every tear has watered the soil for something new to bloom. God has not forgotten you. He has never left you, and He never will.

As you step into what comes next, I pray you carry with you the truth that you are worthy of love, deserving of peace, and destined for joy. May you release what was never meant for you, so your hands are open to receive what God has prepared.

This is not goodbye — it's a new beginning. And I believe with all my heart that your best days are still ahead.

With love,

Shechinahglory E. Tucker

Acknowledgments

First and foremost, I thank God for being my source of strength, wisdom, and love throughout this journey. Without His presence, none of this would be possible.

To my family and loved ones — thank you for supporting me, praying for me, and standing with me as I walked through both shadow and light. Your encouragement gave me the courage to keep writing and sharing my truth.

A special thank you to my mother, whose words continue to echo in my heart: "This book seems like it's going to be very moving. I believe it may answer some questions that are rooted deep in some people's hearts, and emotions some people may be set free from this book. Stay God-focused. Stay transparent, stay true to yourself, but always look for God to do the work in you. He is doing it. I pray that your healing will be complete. I love you, Shechinahglory. I'm proud and excited to see it through."

Your faith in me reminds me daily of why I must keep pressing forward with purpose.

And to every reader holding this book — thank you. May these words meet you right where you are and lead you closer to God's love, healing, and wholeness.

About Shekinahglory Press
About the Publisher

Shekinahglory Press is an independent publishing imprint founded by Shechinahglory Tucker.

With a mission to uplift, heal, and inspire, Shekinahglory Press is devoted to bringing forth

faith-centered and purpose-driven works that empower readers to embrace their divine calling.

For more information, visit: www.shekinahglorypress.com

Email: info@shekinahglorypress.com

Shekinahglory
PRESS